THE WISDOM
OF
MAO TSE-TUNG

PHILOSOPHICAL LIBRARY

New York

Distributed to the Trade by

BOOK SALES INC.

352 Park Ave South

New York, N.Y., 10010

FOREWORD

Mao Tse-Tung, until 1959 chairman of the People's Republic of China, and still chairman of the Central Committee of the Communist Party of China, is the most important single person in China today. For twenty-two years he led Chinese armies in guerrilla warfare against foreign invaders, and then against the Chinese government in an effort to effect a complete socio-political revolution in his country. He succeeded, and has since been the spokesman for one-fourth of the human race.

Mao was born in Shaoshan, Hunan Province, on November 19, 1893. His father was a peasant and Mao began working in the fields at the age of six. After an education gained at great sacrifice, Mao joined the revolutionary army, formed by Sun Yat-sen, an American-educated Chinese who promoted the overthrow of the ruling and despotic Manchus. The subsequent collapse of the Manchu regime gave Mao his first taste of the effects of revolutionary activism and set the stage for his future career.

CONTENTS

On Practice

On the Relation Between Knowledge and Practice,
Between Knowing and Doing   11
Notes   25

On Contradiction

I. The Two World Outlooks   29
II. The Universality of Contradiction   33
III. The Particularity of Contradiction   37
IV. The Principal Contradiction and the Principal
     Aspect of a Contradiction   49
V. The Identity and Struggle of the Aspects of a
     Contradiction   55
VI. The Place of Antagonism in Contradiction   61
VII. Conclusion   63
Notes   64

On New Democracy

I. Whither China?   69
II. We Want to Build a New China   70
III. China's Historical Characteristics   70
IV. The Chinese Revolution is Part of the World
     Revolution   72
V. The Politics of New Democracy   77
VI. The Economy of New Democracy   83
VII. Refutation of Bourgeois Dictatorship   84
VIII. Refutation of "Left" Phrase-Mongering   88
IX. Refutation of the Die-Hards   90
X. The Three People's Principles, Old and New   93
XI. The Culture of New Democracy   99
XII. The Historical Characteristics of China's
     Cultural Revolution   101
XIII. The Four Periods   103
XIV. Some Wrong Ideas About the Nature of Culture   108
XV. A National, Scientific and Mass Culture   110
Notes   112

ON PRACTICE

ON PRACTICE

On the Relation Between Knowledge and Practice, Between Knowing and Doing

July 1937

Before Marx, materialism examined the problem of knowledge apart from the social nature of man and apart from his historical development, and was therefore incapable of understanding the dependence of knowledge on social practice, that is, the dependence of knowledge on production and the class struggle.

Above all, Marxists regard man's activity in production as the most fundamental practical activity, the determinant of all his other activities. Man's knowledge depends mainly on his activity in material production, through which he comes gradually to understand the phenomena, the properties and the laws of nature, and the relations between himself and nature; and through his activity in production he also gradually comes to understand, in varying degrees, certain relations that exist between man and man. None of this knowledge can be acquired apart from activity in production. In a classless society every person, as a member of society, joins in common effort with the other members, enters into definite relations of production with them and engages in production to meet man's material needs. In all class societies, the members of the different social classes also enter, in different ways, into definite relations of production and

There used to be a number of comrades in our Party who were dogmatists and who for a long period rejected the experience of the Chinese revolution, denying the truth that "Marxism is not a dogma but a guide to action" and overawing people with words and phrases from Marxist works, torn out of context. There were also a number of comrades who were empiricists and who for a long period restricted themselves to their own fragmentary experience and did not understand the importance of theory for revolutionary practice or see the revolution as a whole, but worked blindly though industriously. The erroneous ideas of these two types of comrades, and particularly of the dogmatists, caused enormous losses to the

11

engage in production to meet their material needs. This is the primary source from which human knowledge develops.

Man's social practice is not confined to activity in production, but takes many other forms — class struggle, political life, scientific and artistic pursuits; in short, as a social being, man participates in all spheres of the practical life of society. Thus man, in varying degrees, comes to know the different relations between man and man, not only through his material life but also through his political and cultural life (both of which are intimately bound up with material life). Of these other types of social practice, class struggle in particular, in all its various forms, exerts a profound influence on the development of man's knowledge. In class society everyone lives as a member of a particular class, and every kind of thinking, without exception, is stamped with the brand of a class.

Marxists hold that in human society activity in production develops step by step from a lower to a higher level and that consequently man's knowledge, whether of nature or of society, also develops step by step from a lower to a higher level, that is, from the shallower to the deeper, from the one-sided to the many-sided. For a very long period in history, men were necessarily confined to a one-sided understanding of the history of society because, for one thing, the bias of the exploiting classes always distorted history and, for another, the small scale of production limited man's outlook. It was not until the modern proletariat emerged along with immense forces of production (large-scale industry) that man was able to acquire a comprehensive, historical understanding of the development of society and turn this knowledge into a science, the science of Marxism.

Marxists hold that man's social practice alone is the criterion of the truth of his knowledge of the external world. What actually happens is that man's knowledge is verified only when he achieves the anticipated results in the process of social practice (material production, class struggle or scientific experiment). If a man wants to succeed in his work, that is, to achieve the anticipated results,

Chinese revolution during 1931-34, and yet the dogmatists, cloaking themselves as Marxists, confused a great many comrades. "On Practice" was written in order to expose the subjectivist errors of dogmatism and empiricism in the Party, and especially the error of dogmatism, from the standpoint of the Marxist theory of knowledge. It was entitled "On Practice" because its stress was on exposing the dogmatist kind of subjectivism, which belittles practice. The ideas contained in this essay were presented by Comrade Mao Tse-tung in a lecture at the Anti-Japanese Military and Political College in Yenan.

he must bring his ideas into correspondence with the laws of the objective external world; if they do not correspond, he will fail in his practice. After he fails, he draws his lessons, corrects his ideas to make them correspond to the laws of the external world, and can thus turn failure into success; this is what is meant by "failure is the mother of success" and "a fall into the pit, a gain in your wit". The dialectical-materialist theory of knowledge places practice in the primary position, holding that human knowledge can in no way be separated from practice and repudiating all the erroneous theories which deny the importance of practice or separate knowledge from practice. Thus Lenin said, "*Practice is higher than (theoretical) knowledge*, for it has not only the dignity of universality, but also of immediate actuality."[1] The Marxist philosophy of dialectical materialism has two outstanding characteristics. One is its class nature: it openly avows that dialectical materialism is in the service of the proletariat. The other is its practicality: it emphasizes the dependence of theory on practice, emphasizes that theory is based on practice and in turn serves practice. The truth of any knowledge or theory is determined not by subjective feelings, but by objective results in social practice. Only social practice can be the criterion of truth. The standpoint of practice is the primary and basic standpoint in the dialectical-materialist theory of knowledge.[2]

But how then does human knowledge arise from practice and in turn serve practice? This will become clear if we look at the process of development of knowledge.

In the process of practice, man at first sees only the phenomenal side, the separate aspects, the external relations of things. For instance, some people from outside come to Yenan on a tour of observation. In the first day or two, they see its topography, streets and houses; they meet many people, attend banquets, evening parties and mass meetings, hear talk of various kinds and read various documents, all these being the phenomena, the separate aspects and the external relations of things. This is called the perceptual stage of cognition, namely, the stage of sense perceptions and impressions. That is, these particular things in Yenan act on the sense organs of the members of the observation group, evoke sense perceptions and give rise in their brains to many impressions together with a rough sketch of the external relations among these impressions: this is the first stage of cognition. At this stage, man cannot as yet form concepts, which are deeper, or draw logical conclusions.

As social practice continues, things that give rise to man's sense perceptions and impressions in the course of his practice are repeated many times; then a sudden change (leap) takes place in the brain in the process of cognition, and concepts are formed. Concepts are no longer the phenomena, the separate aspects and the external relations of things; they grasp the essence, the totality and the internal relations of things. Between concepts and sense perceptions there is not only a quantitative but also a qualitative difference. Proceeding further, by means of judgement and inference one is able to draw logical conclusions. The expression in *San Kuo Yen Yi*,[3] "knit the brows and a stratagem comes to mind", or in everyday language, "let me think it over", refers to man's use of concepts in the brain to form judgements and inferences. This is the second stage of cognition. When the members of the observation group have collected various data and, what is more, have "thought them over", they are able to arrive at the judgement that "the Communist Party's policy of the National United Front Against Japan is thorough, sincere and genuine". Having made this judgement, they can, if they too are genuine about uniting to save the nation, go a step further and draw the following conclusion, "The National United Front Against Japan can succeed." This stage of conception, judgement and inference is the more important stage in the entire process of knowing a thing; it is the stage of rational knowledge. The real task of knowing is, through perception, to arrive at thought, to arrive step by step at the comprehension of the internal contradictions of objective things, of their laws and of the internal relations between one process and another, that is, to arrive at logical knowledge. To repeat, logical knowledge differs from perceptual knowledge in that perceptual knowledge pertains to the separate aspects, the phenomena and the external relations of things, whereas logical knowledge takes a big stride forward to reach the totality, the essence and the internal relations of things and discloses the inner contradictions in the surrounding world. Therefore, logical knowledge is capable of grasping the development of the surrounding world in its totality, in the internal relations of all its aspects.

This dialectical-materialist theory of the process of development of knowledge, basing itself on practice and proceeding from the shallower to the deeper, was never worked out by anybody before the rise of Marxism. Marxist materialism solved this problem correctly for the first time, pointing out both materialistically and dialectically

14

the deepening movement of cognition, the movement by which man in society progresses from perceptual knowledge to logical knowledge in his complex, constantly recurring practice of production and class struggle. Lenin said, "The abstraction of *matter*, of a *law* of nature, the abstraction of *value*, etc., in short, *all* scientific (correct, serious, not absurd) abstractions reflect nature more deeply, truly and *completely*."[4] Marxism-Leninism holds that each of the two stages in the process of cognition has its own characteristics, with knowledge manifesting itself as perceptual at the lower stage and logical at the higher stage, but that both are stages in an integrated process of cognition. The perceptual and the rational are qualitatively different, but are not divorced from each other; they are unified on the basis of practice. Our practice proves that what is perceived cannot at once be comprehended and that only what is comprehended can be more deeply perceived. Perception only solves the problem of phenomena; theory alone can solve the problem of essence. The solving of both these problems is not separable in the slightest degree from practice. Whoever wants to know a thing has no way of doing so except by coming into contact with it, that is, by living (practising) in its environment. In feudal society it was impossible to know the laws of capitalist society in advance because capitalism had not yet emerged, the relevant practice was lacking. Marxism could be the product only of capitalist society. Marx, in the era of laissez-faire capitalism, could not concretely know certain laws peculiar to the era of imperialism beforehand, because imperialism, the last stage of capitalism, had not yet emerged and the relevant practice was lacking; only Lenin and Stalin could undertake this task. Leaving aside their genius, the reason why Marx, Engels, Lenin and Stalin could work out their theories was mainly that they personally took part in the practice of the class struggle and the scientific experimentation of their time; lacking this condition, no genius could have succeeded. The saying, "without stepping outside his gate the scholar knows all the wide world's affairs", was mere empty talk in past times when technology was undeveloped. Even though this saying can be valid in the present age of developed technology, the people with real personal knowledge are those engaged in practice the wide world over. And it is only when these people have come to "know" through their practice and when their knowledge has reached him through writing and technical media that the "scholar" can indirectly "know all the wide world's affairs". If you want to know a certain thing or a certain class of things directly, you must personally participate in the practical struggle to change reality, to change that thing or class of things, for only thus can you come into contact with them as phenomena; only through personal participation in the practical struggle to change reality can you uncover the essence of that thing or class of things and comprehend them. This is the path to knowledge which every man actually travels, though some people, deliberately distorting matters, argue to the contrary. The most ridiculous person in the world is the "know-all" who picks up a smattering of hearsay knowledge and proclaims himself "the world's Number One authority"; this merely shows that he has not taken a proper measure of himself. Knowledge is a matter of science, and no dishonesty or conceit whatsoever is permissible. What is required is definitely the reverse — honesty and modesty. If you want knowledge, you must take part in the practice of changing reality. If you want to know the taste of a pear, you must change the pear by eating it yourself. If you want to know the structure and properties of the atom, you must make physical and chemical experiments to change the state of the atom. If you want to know the theory and methods of revolution, you must take part in revolution. All genuine knowledge originates in direct experience. But one cannot have direct experience of everything; as a matter of fact, most of our knowledge comes from indirect experience, for example, all knowledge from past times and foreign lands. To our ancestors and to foreigners, such knowledge was — or is — a matter of direct experience, and this knowledge is reliable if in the course of their direct experience the requirement of "scientific abstraction", spoken of by Lenin, was — or is — fulfilled and objective reality scientifically reflected, otherwise it is not reliable. Hence a man's knowledge consists only of two parts, that which comes from direct experience and that which comes from indirect experience. Moreover, what is indirect experience for me is direct experience for other people. Consequently, considered as a whole, knowledge of any kind is inseparable from direct experience. All knowledge originates in perception of the objective external world through man's physical sense organs. Anyone who denies such perception, denies direct experience, or denies personal participation in the practice that changes reality, is not a materialist. That is why the "know-all" is ridiculous. There is an old Chinese saying, "How can you catch tiger cubs without entering the tiger's lair?" This saying holds true for man's practice and it

16

also holds true for the theory of knowledge. There can be no knowledge apart from practice.

To make clear the dialectical-materialist movement of cognition arising on the basis of the practice which changes reality — to make clear the gradually deepening movement of cognition — a few additional concrete examples are given below.

In its knowledge of capitalist society, the proletariat was only in the perceptual stage of cognition in the first period of its practice, the period of machine-smashing and spontaneous struggle; it knew only some of the aspects and the external relations of the phenomena of capitalism. The proletariat was then still a "class-in-itself". But when it reached the second period of its practice, the period of conscious and organized economic and political struggles, the proletariat was able to comprehend the essence of capitalist society, the relations of exploitation between social classes and its own historical task; and it was able to do so because of its own practice and because of its experience of prolonged struggle, which Marx and Engels scientifically summed up in all its variety to create the theory of Marxism for the education of the proletariat. It was then that the proletariat became a "class-for-itself".

Similarly with the Chinese people's knowledge of imperialism. The first stage was one of superficial, perceptual knowledge, as shown in the indiscriminate anti-foreign struggles of the Movement of the Taiping Heavenly Kingdom, the Yi Ho Tuan Movement, and so on. It was only in the second stage that the Chinese people reached the stage of rational knowledge, saw the internal and external contradictions of imperialism and saw the essential truth that imperialism had allied itself with China's comprador and feudal classes to oppress and exploit the great masses of the Chinese people. This knowledge began about the time of the May 4th Movement of 1919.

Next, let us consider war. If those who lead a war lack experience of war, then at the initial stage they will not understand the profound laws pertaining to the directing of a specific war (such as our Agrarian Revolutionary War of the past decade). At the initial stage they will merely experience a good deal of fighting and, what is more, suffer many defeats. But this experience (the experience of battles won and especially of battles lost) enables them to comprehend the inner thread of the whole war, namely, the laws of that specific war, to understand its strategy and tactics, and consequently to direct

17

the war with confidence. If, at such a moment, the command is turned over to an inexperienced person, then he too will have to suffer a number of defeats (gain experience) before he can comprehend the true laws of the war.

"I am not sure I can handle it." We often hear this remark when a comrade hesitates to accept an assignment. Why is he unsure of himself? Because he has no systematic understanding of the content and circumstances of the assignment, or because he has had little or no contact with such work, and so the laws governing it are beyond him. After a detailed analysis of the nature and circumstances of the assignment, he will feel more sure of himself and do it willingly. If he spends some time at the job and gains experience and if he is a person who is willing to look into matters with an open mind and not one who approaches problems subjectively, one-sidedly and superficially, then he can draw conclusions for himself as to how to go about the job and do it with much more courage. Only those who are subjective, one-sided and superficial in their approach to problems will smugly issue orders or directives the moment they arrive on the scene, without considering the circumstances, without viewing things in their totality (their history and their present state as a whole) and without getting to the essence of things (their nature and the internal relations between one thing and another). Such people are bound to trip and fall.

Thus it can be seen that the first step in the process of cognition is contact with the objects of the external world; this belongs to the stage of perception. The second step is to synthesize the data of perception by arranging and reconstructing them; this belongs to the stage of conception, judgement and inference. It is only when the data of perception are very rich (not fragmentary) and correspond to reality (are not illusory) that they can be the basis for forming correct concepts and theories.

Here two important points must be emphasized. The first, which has been stated before but should be repeated here, is the dependence of rational knowledge upon perceptual knowledge. Anyone who thinks that rational knowledge need not be derived from perceptual knowledge is an idealist. In the history of philosophy there is the "rationalist" school that admits the reality only of reason and not of experience, believing that reason alone is reliable while perceptual experience is not; this school errs by turning things upside down. The rational is reliable precisely because it has its source in sense perceptions, otherwise it would be like water without a source, a tree without roots, subjective, self-engendered and unreliable. As to the sequence in the process of cognition, perceptual experience comes first; we stress the significance of social practice in the process of cognition precisely because social practice alone can give rise to human knowledge and it alone can start man on the acquisition of perceptual experience from the objective world. For a person who shuts his eyes, stops his ears and totally cuts himself off from the objective world there can be no such thing as knowledge. Knowledge begins with experience — this is the materialism of the theory of knowledge.

The second point is that knowledge needs to be deepened, that the perceptual stage of knowledge needs to be developed to the rational stage — this is the dialectics of the theory of knowledge.[5] To think that knowledge can stop at the lower, perceptual stage and that perceptual knowledge alone is reliable while rational knowledge is not, would be to repeat the historical error of "empiricism". This theory errs in failing to understand that, although the data of perception reflect certain realities in the objective world (I am not speaking here of idealist empiricism which confines experience to so-called introspection), they are merely one-sided and superficial, reflecting things incompletely and not reflecting their essence. Fully to reflect a thing in its totality, to reflect its essence, to reflect its inherent laws, it is necessary through the exercise of thought to reconstruct the rich data of sense perception, discarding the dross and selecting the essential, eliminating the false and retaining the true, proceeding from the one to the other and from the outside to the inside, in order to form a system of concepts and theories — it is necessary to make a leap from perceptual to rational knowledge. Such reconstructed knowledge is not more empty or more unreliable; on the contrary, whatever has been scientifically reconstructed in the process of cognition, on the basis of practice, reflects objective reality, as Lenin said, more deeply, more truly, more fully. As against this, vulgar "practical men" respect experience but despise theory, and therefore cannot have a comprehensive view of an entire objective process, lack clear direction and long-range perspective, and are complacent over occasional successes and glimpses of the truth. If such persons direct a revolution, they will lead it up a blind alley.

Rational knowledge depends upon perceptual knowledge and perceptual knowledge remains to be developed into rational knowledge — this is the dialectical-materialist theory of knowledge. In philosophy, neither "rationalism" nor "empiricism" understands the historical or the dialectical nature of knowledge, and although each of these schools contains one aspect of the truth (here I am referring to materialist, not to idealist, rationalism and empiricism), both are wrong on the theory of knowledge as a whole. The dialectical-materialist movement of knowledge from the perceptual to the rational holds true for a minor process of cognition (for instance, knowing a single thing or task) as well as for a major process of cognition (for instance, knowing a whole society or a revolution).

But the movement of knowledge does not end here. If the dialectical-materialist movement of knowledge were to stop at rational knowledge, only half the problem would be dealt with. And as far as Marxist philosophy is concerned, only the less important half at that. Marxist philosophy holds that the most important problem does not lie in understanding the laws of the objective world and thus being able to explain it, but in applying the knowledge of these laws actively to change the world. From the Marxist viewpoint, theory is important, and its importance is fully expressed in Lenin's statement, "Without revolutionary theory there can be no revolutionary movement."[6] But Marxism emphasizes the importance of theory precisely and only because it can guide action. If we have a correct theory but merely prate about it, pigeonhole it and do not put it into practice, then that theory, however good, is of no significance. Knowledge begins with practice, and theoretical knowledge is acquired through practice and must then return to practice. The active function of knowledge manifests itself not only in the active leap from perceptual to rational knowledge, but — and this is more important — it must manifest itself in the leap from rational knowledge to revolutionary practice. The knowledge which grasps the laws of the world, must be redirected to the practice of changing the world, must be applied anew in the practice of production, in the practice of revolutionary class struggle and revolutionary national struggle and in the practice of scientific experiment. This is the process of testing and developing theory, the continuation of the whole process of cognition. The problem of whether theory corresponds to objective reality is not, and cannot be, completely solved in the movement of knowledge from the perceptual to the rational, mentioned above. The only way to solve this problem completely is to redirect rational knowledge to social practice, apply theory to practice and see whether it can achieve the objectives one has in mind. Many theories of natural science are held to be true not only because they were so considered when natural scientists originated them, but because they have been verified in subsequent scientific practice. Similarly, Marxism-Leninism is held to be true not only because it was so considered when it was scientifically formulated by Marx, Engels, Lenin and Stalin but because it has been verified in the subsequent practice of revolutionary class struggle and revolutionary national struggle. Dialectical materialism is universally true because it is impossible for anyone to escape from its domain in his practice. The history of human knowledge tells us that the truth of many theories is incomplete and that this incompleteness is remedied through the test of practice. Many theories are erroneous and it is through the test of practice that their errors are corrected. That is why practice is the criterion of truth and why "the standpoint of life, of practice, should be first and fundamental in the theory of knowledge".[7] Stalin has well said, "Theory becomes purposeless if it is not connected with revolutionary practice, just as practice gropes in the dark if its path is not illumined by revolutionary theory."[8]

When we get to this point, is the movement of knowledge completed? Our answer is: it is and yet it is not. When men in society throw themselves into the practice of changing a certain objective process (whether natural or social) at a certain stage of its development, they can, as a result of the reflection of the objective process in their brains and the exercise of their subjective activity, advance their knowledge from the perceptual to the rational, and create ideas, theories, plans or programmes which correspond in general to the laws of that objective process. They then apply these ideas, theories, plans or programmes in practice in the same objective process. And if they can realize the aims they have in mind, that is, if in that same process of practice they can translate, or on the whole translate, those previously formulated ideas, theories, plans or programmes into fact, then the movement of knowledge may be considered completed with regard to this particular process. In the process of changing nature, take for example the fulfilment of an engineering plan, the verification of a scientific hypothesis, the manufacture of an implement or the reaping of a crop; or in the process of changing society, take for example the victory of a strike, victory in a war or the fulfilment of an educational plan. All these may be considered the realization of aims one has in mind. But generally speaking, whether in the practice of changing nature or of changing society, men's original ideas, theories, plans or programmes are seldom realized without any alteration.

21

This is because people engaged in changing reality are usually subject to numerous limitations; they are limited not only by existing scientific and technological conditions but also by the development of the objective process itself and the degree to which this process has become manifest (the aspects and the essence of the objective process have not yet been fully revealed). In such a situation, ideas, theories, plans or programmes are usually altered partially and sometimes even wholly, because of the discovery of unforeseen circumstances in the course of practice. That is to say, it does happen that the original ideas, theories, plans or programmes fail to correspond with reality either in whole or in part and are wholly or partially incorrect. In many instances, failures have to be repeated many times before errors in knowledge can be corrected and correspondence with the laws of the objective process achieved, and consequently before the subjective can be transformed into the objective, or in other words, before the anticipated results can be achieved in practice. But when that point is reached, no matter how, the movement of human knowledge regarding a certain objective process at a certain stage of its development may be considered completed.

However, so far as the progression of the process is concerned, the movement of human knowledge is not completed. Every process, whether in the realm of nature or of society, progresses and develops by reason of its internal contradiction and struggle, and the movement of human knowledge should also progress and develop along with it. As far as social movements are concerned, true revolutionary leaders must not only be good at correcting their ideas, theories, plans or programmes when errors are discovered, as has been indicated above; but when a certain objective process has already progressed and changed from one stage of development to another, they must also be good at making themselves and all their fellow-revolutionaries progress and change in their subjective knowledge along with it, that is to say, they must ensure that the proposed new revolutionary tasks and new working programmes correspond to the new changes in the situation. In a revolutionary period the situation changes very rapidly; if the knowledge of revolutionaries does not change rapidly in accordance with the changed situation, they will be unable to lead the revolution to victory.

It often happens, however, that thinking lags behind reality; this is because man's cognition is limited by numerous social conditions. We are opposed to die-hards in the revolutionary ranks whose thinking fails to advance with changing objective circumstances and has manifested itself historically as Right opportunism. These people fail to see that the struggle of opposites has already pushed the objective process forward while their knowledge has stopped at the old stage. This is characteristic of the thinking of all die-hards. Their thinking is divorced from social practice, and they cannot march ahead to guide the chariot of society; they simply trail behind, grumbling that it goes too fast and trying to drag it back or turn it in the opposite direction.

We are also opposed to "Left" phrase-mongering. The thinking of "Leftists" outstrips a given stage of development of the objective process; some regard their fantasies as truth, while others strain to realize in the present an ideal which can only be realized in the future. They alienate themselves from the current practice of the majority of the people and from the realities of the day, and show themselves adventurist in their actions.

Idealism and mechanical materialism, opportunism and adventurism, are all characterized by the breach between the subjective and the objective, by the separation of knowledge from practice. The Marxist-Leninist theory of knowledge, characterized as it is by scientific social practice, cannot but resolutely oppose these wrong ideologies. Marxists recognize that in the absolute and general process of development of the universe, the development of each particular process is relative, and that hence, in the endless flow of absolute truth, man's knowledge of a particular process at any given stage of development is only relative truth. The sum total of innumerable relative truths constitutes absolute truth.[9] The development of an objective process is full of contradictions and struggles, and so is the development of the movement of human knowledge. All the dialectical movements of the objective world can sooner or later be reflected in human knowledge. In social practice, the process of coming into being, developing and passing away is infinite, and so is the process of coming into being, developing and passing away in human knowledge. As man's practice which changes objective reality in accordance with given ideas, theories, plans or programmes, advances further and further, his knowledge of objective reality likewise becomes deeper and deeper. The movement of change in the world of objective reality is never-ending and so is man's cognition of truth through practice. Marxism-Leninism has in no way exhausted truth but ceaselessly opens up roads to the knowledge of truth in the course

23

of practice. Our conclusion is the concrete, historical unity of the subjective and the objective, of theory and practice, of knowing and doing, and we are opposed to all erroneous ideologies, whether "Left" or Right, which depart from concrete history.

In the present epoch of the development of society, the responsibility of correctly knowing and changing the world has been placed by history upon the shoulders of the proletariat and its party. This process, the practice of changing the world, which is determined in accordance with scientific knowledge, has already reached a historic moment in the world and in China, a great moment unprecedented in human history, that is, the moment for completely banishing darkness from the world and from China and for changing the world into a world of light such as never previously existed. The struggle of the proletariat and the revolutionary people to change the world comprises the fulfilment of the following tasks: to change the objective world and, at the same time, their own subjective world — to change their cognitive ability and change the relations between the subjective and the objective world. Such a change has already come about in one part of the globe, in the Soviet Union. There the people are pushing forward this process of change. The people of China and the rest of the world either are going through, or will go through, such a process. And the objective world which is to be changed also includes all the opponents of change, who, in order to be changed, must go through a stage of compulsion before they can enter the stage of voluntary, conscious change. The epoch of world communism will be reached when all mankind voluntarily and consciously changes itself and the world.

Discover the truth through practice, and again through practice verify and develop the truth. Start from perceptual knowledge and actively develop it into rational knowledge; then start from rational knowledge and actively guide revolutionary practice to change both the subjective and the objective world. Practice, knowledge, again practice, and again knowledge. This form repeats itself in endless cycles, and with each cycle the content of practice and knowledge rises to a higher level. Such is the whole of the dialectical-materialist theory of knowledge, and such is the dialectical-materialist theory of the unity of knowing and doing.

NOTES

[1] V. I. Lenin, "Conspectus of Hegel's *The Science of Logic*", *Collected Works*, Russ. ed., Moscow, 1958, Vol. XXXVIII, p. 205.

[2] See Karl Marx, "Theses on Feuerbach", Karl Marx and Frederick Engels, *Selected Works*, in two volumes, Eng. ed., FLPH, Moscow, 1958, Vol. II, p. 403, and V. I. Lenin, *Materialism and Empirio-Criticism*, Eng. ed., FLPH, Moscow, 1952, pp. 136-42.

[3] *San Kuo Yen Yi (Tales of the Three Kingdoms)* is a famous Chinese historical novel by Lo Kuan-chung (late 14th and early 15th century).

[4] V. I. Lenin, "Conspectus of Hegel's *The Science of Logic*", *Collected Works*, Russ. ed., Moscow, 1958, Vol. XXXVIII, p. 161.

[5] "In order to understand, it is necessary empirically to begin understanding, study, to rise from empiricism to the universal." (*Ibid.*, p. 197.)

[6] V. I. Lenin, "What Is to Be Done?", *Collected Works*, Eng. ed., FLPH, Moscow, 1961, Vol. V, p. 369.

[7] V. I. Lenin, *Materialism and Empirio-Criticism*, Eng. ed., FLPH, Moscow, 1952, p. 141.

[8] J. V. Stalin, "The Foundations of Leninism", *Problems of Leninism*, Eng. ed., FLPH, Moscow, 1954, p. 31.

[9] See V. I. Lenin, *Materialism and Empirio-Criticism*, Eng. ed., FLPH, Moscow, 1952, pp. 129-36.

ON CONTRADICTION

ON CONTRADICTION

August 1937

The law of contradiction in things, that is, the law of the unity of opposites, is the basic law of materialist dialectics. Lenin said, "Dialectics in the proper sense is the study of contradiction *in the very essence of objects*."[1] Lenin often called this law the essence of dialectics; he also called it the kernel of dialectics.[2] In studying this law, therefore, we cannot but touch upon a variety of questions, upon a number of philosophical problems. If we can become clear on all these problems, we shall arrive at a fundamental understanding of materialist dialectics. The problems are: the two world outlooks, the universality of contradiction, the particularity of contradiction, the principal contradiction and the principal aspect of a contradiction, the identity and struggle of the aspects of a contradiction, and the place of antagonism in contradiction.

The criticism to which the idealism of the Deborin school has been subjected in Soviet philosophical circles in recent years has aroused great interest among us. Deborin's idealism has exerted a very bad influence in the Chinese Communist Party, and it cannot be said that the dogmatist thinking in our Party is unrelated to the approach of that school. Our present study of philosophy should therefore have the eradication of dogmatist thinking as its main objective.

I. THE TWO WORLD OUTLOOKS

Throughout the history of human knowledge, there have been two conceptions concerning the law of development of the universe, the

This essay on philosophy was written by Comrade Mao Tse-tung after his essay "On Practice" and with the same object of overcoming the serious error of dogmatist thinking to be found in the Party at the time. Originally delivered as lectures at the Anti-Japanese Military and Political College in Yenan, it was revised by the author on its inclusion in his *Selected Works*.

metaphysical conception and the dialectical conception, which form two opposing world outlooks. Lenin said:

> The two basic (or two possible? or two historically observable?) conceptions of development (evolution) are: development as decrease and increase, as repetition, *and* development as a unity of opposites (the division of a unity into mutually exclusive opposites and their reciprocal relation).[3]

Here Lenin was referring to these two different world outlooks.

In China another name for metaphysics is *hsuan-hsueh*. For a long period in history whether in China or in Europe, this way of thinking, which is part and parcel of the idealist world outlook, occupied a dominant position in human thought. In Europe, the materialism of the bourgeoisie in its early days was also metaphysical. As the social economy of many European countries advanced to the stage of highly developed capitalism, as the forces of production, the class struggle and the sciences developed to a level unprecedented in history, and as the industrial proletariat became the greatest motive force in historical development, there arose the Marxist world outlook of materialist dialectics. Then, in addition to open and barefaced reactionary idealism, vulgar evolutionism emerged among the bourgeoisie to oppose materialist dialectics.

The metaphysical or vulgar evolutionist world outlook sees things as isolated, static and one-sided. It regards all things in the universe, their forms and their species, as eternally isolated from one another and immutable. Such change as there is can only be an increase or decrease in quantity or a change of place. Moreover, the cause of such an increase or decrease or change of place is not inside things but outside them, that is, the motive force is external. Metaphysicians hold that all the different kinds of things in the universe and all their characteristics have been the same ever since they first came into being. All subsequent changes have simply been increases or decreases in quantity. They contend that a thing can only keep on repeating itself as the same kind of thing and cannot change into anything different. In their opinion, capitalist exploitation, capitalist competition, the individualist ideology of capitalist society, and so on, can all be found in ancient slave society, or even in primitive society, and will exist for ever unchanged. They ascribe the causes of social development to factors external to society, such as geography and climate. They search in an over-simplified way outside a thing for the causes of its development, and they deny the theory of materialist dialectics which holds that development arises from the contradictions inside a thing. Consequently they can explain neither the qualitative diversity of things, nor the phenomenon of one quality changing into another. In Europe, this mode of thinking existed as mechanical materialism in the 17th and 18th centuries and as vulgar evolutionism at the end of the 19th and the beginning of the 20th centuries. In China, there was the metaphysical thinking exemplified in the saying "Heaven changeth not, likewise the Tao changeth not",[4] and it was supported by the decadent feudal ruling classes for a long time. Mechanical materialism and vulgar evolutionism, which were imported from Europe in the last hundred years, are supported by the bourgeoisie.

As opposed to the metaphysical world outlook, the world outlook of materialist dialectics holds that in order to understand the development of a thing we should study it internally and in its relations with other things; in other words, the development of things should be seen as their internal and necessary self-movement, while each thing in its movement is interrelated with and interacts on the things around it. The fundamental cause of the development of a thing is not external but internal; it lies in the contradictoriness within the thing. There is internal contradiction in every single thing, hence its motion and development. Contradictoriness within a thing is the fundamental cause of its development, while its interrelations and interactions with other things are secondary causes. Thus materialist dialectics effectively combats the theory of external causes, or of an external motive force, advanced by metaphysical mechanical materialism and vulgar evolutionism. It is evident that purely external causes can only give rise to mechanical motion, that is, to changes in scale or quantity, but cannot explain why things differ qualitatively in thousands of ways and why one thing changes into another. As a matter of fact, even mechanical motion under external force occurs through the internal contradictoriness of things. Simple growth in plants and animals, their quantitative development, is likewise chiefly the result of their internal contradictions. Similarly, social development is due chiefly not to external but to internal causes. Countries with almost the same geographical and climatic conditions display great diversity and unevenness in their development. Moreover, great social changes may take place in one and the same country although its geography and climate remain unchanged. Imperialist Russia changed into the socialist Soviet Union, and feudal Japan, which had locked its doors against

31

the world, changed into imperialist Japan, although no change occurred in the geography and climate of either country. Long dominated by feudalism, China has undergone great changes in the last hundred years and is now changing in the direction of a new China, liberated and free, and yet no change has occurred in her geography and climate. Changes do take place in the geography and climate of the earth as a whole and in every part of it, but they are insignificant when compared with changes in society; geographical and climatic changes manifest themselves in terms of tens of thousands of years, while social changes manifest themselves in thousands, hundreds or tens of years, and even in a few years or months in times of revolution. According to materialist dialectics, changes in nature are due chiefly to the development of the internal contradictions in nature. Changes in society are due chiefly to the development of the internal contradictions in society, that is, the contradiction between the productive forces and the relations of production, the contradiction between classes and the contradiction between the old and the new; it is the development of these contradictions that pushes society forward and gives the impetus for the supersession of the old society by the new. Does materialist dialectics exclude external causes? Not at all. It holds that external causes are the condition of change and internal causes are the basis of change, and that external causes become operative through internal causes. In a suitable temperature an egg changes into a chicken, but no temperature can change a stone into a chicken, because each has a different basis. There is constant interaction between the peoples of different countries. In the era of capitalism, and especially in the era of imperialism and proletarian revolution, the interaction and mutual impact of different countries in the political, economic and cultural spheres are extremely great. The October Socialist Revolution ushered in a new epoch in world history as well as in Russian history. It exerted influence on internal changes in the other countries in the world and, similarly and in a particularly profound way, on internal changes in China. These changes, however, were effected through the inner laws of development of these countries, China included. In battle, one army is victorious and the other is defeated; both the victory and the defeat are determined by internal causes. The one is victorious either because it is strong or because of its competent generalship, the other is vanquished either because it is weak or because of its incompetent generalship; it is through internal causes that external causes become operative. In China in 1927, the defeat of the proletariat by the big bourgeoisie came about through the opportunism then to be found within the Chinese proletariat itself (inside the Chinese Communist Party). When we liquidated this opportunism, the Chinese revolution resumed its advance. Later, the Chinese revolution again suffered severe setbacks at the hands of the enemy, because adventurism had risen within our Party. When we liquidated this adventurism, our cause advanced once again. Thus it can be seen that to lead the revolution to victory, a political party must depend on the correctness of its own political line and the solidity of its own organization.

The dialectical world outlook emerged in ancient times both in China and in Europe. Ancient dialectics, however, had a somewhat spontaneous and naive character; in the social and historical conditions then prevailing, it was not yet able to form a theoretical system, hence it could not fully explain the world and was supplanted by metaphysics. The famous German philosopher Hegel, who lived in the late 18th and early 19th centuries, made most important contributions to dialectics, but his dialectics was idealist. It was not until Marx and Engels, the great protagonists of the proletarian movement, had synthesized the positive achievements in the history of human knowledge and, in particular, critically absorbed the rational elements of Hegelian dialectics and created the great theory of dialectical and historical materialism that an unprecedented revolution occurred in the history of human knowledge. This theory was further developed by Lenin and Stalin. As soon as it spread to China, it wrought tremendous changes in the world of Chinese thought.

This dialectical world outlook teaches us primarily how to observe and analyse the movement of opposites in different things and, on the basis of such analysis, to indicate the methods for resolving contradictions. It is therefore most important for us to understand the law of contradiction in things in a concrete way.

II. THE UNIVERSALITY OF CONTRADICTION

For convenience of exposition, I shall deal first with the universality of contradiction and then proceed to the particularity of contradiction. The reason is that the universality of contradiction can be explained more briefly, for it has been widely recognized ever since

33

the materialist-dialectical world outlook was discovered and materialist dialectics applied with outstanding success to analysing many aspects of human history and natural history and to changing many aspects of society and nature (as in the Soviet Union) by the great creators and continuers of Marxism — Marx, Engels, Lenin and Stalin; whereas the particularity of contradiction is still not clearly understood by many comrades, and especially by the dogmatists. They do not understand that it is precisely in the particularity of contradiction that the universality of contradiction resides. Nor do they understand how important is the study of the particularity of contradiction in the concrete things confronting us for guiding the course of revolutionary practice. Therefore, it is necessary to stress the study of the particularity of contradiction and to explain it at adequate length. For this reason, in our analysis of the law of contradiction in things, we shall first analyse the universality of contradiction, then place special stress on analysing the particularity of contradiction, and finally return to the universality of contradiction.

The universality or absoluteness of contradiction has a twofold meaning. One is that contradiction exists in the process of development of all things, and the other is that in the process of development of each thing a movement of opposites exists from beginning to end.

Engels said, "Motion itself is a contradiction."[5] Lenin defined the law of the unity of opposites as "the recognition (discovery) of the contradictory, *mutually exclusive*, opposite tendencies in *all* phenomena and processes of nature (*including* mind and society)".[6] Are these ideas correct? Yes, they are. The interdependence of the contradictory aspects present in all things and the struggle between these aspects determine the life of all things and push their development forward. There is nothing that does not contain contradiction; without contradiction nothing would exist.

Contradiction is the basis of the simple forms of motion (for instance, mechanical motion) and still more so of the complex forms of motion.

Engels explained the universality of contradiction as follows:

> If simple mechanical change of place contains a contradiction, this is even more true of the higher forms of motion of matter, and especially of organic life and its development. . . . life consists precisely and primarily in this — that a being is at each moment itself and yet something else. Life is therefore also a contradiction

34

which is present in things and processes themselves, and which constantly originates and resolves itself; and as soon as the contradiction ceases, life, too, comes to an end, and death steps in. We likewise saw that also in the sphere of thought we could not escape contradictions, and that for example the contradiction between man's inherently unlimited capacity for knowledge and its actual presence only in men who are externally limited and possess limited cognition finds its solution in what is — at least practically, for us — an endless succession of generations, in infinite progress.

. . . one of the basic principles of higher mathematics is the contradiction that in certain circumstances straight lines and curves may be the same. . . .

But even lower mathematics teems with contradictions.[7]

Lenin illustrated the universality of contradiction as follows:

In mathematics: + and —. Differential and integral.
In mechanics: action and reaction.
In physics: positive and negative electricity.
In chemistry: the combination and dissociation of atoms.
In social science: the class struggle.[8]

In war, offence and defence, advance and retreat, victory and defeat are all mutually contradictory phenomena. One cannot exist without the other. The two aspects are at once in conflict and in interdependence, and this constitutes the totality of a war, pushes its development forward and solves its problems.

Every difference in men's concepts should be regarded as reflecting an objective contradiction. Objective contradictions are reflected in subjective thinking, and this process constitutes the contradictory movement of concepts, pushes forward the development of thought, and ceaselessly solves problems in man's thinking.

Opposition and struggle between ideas of different kinds constantly occur within the Party; this is a reflection within the Party of contradictions between classes and between the new and the old in society. If there were no contradictions in the Party and no ideological struggles to resolve them, the Party's life would come to an end.

Thus it is already clear that contradiction exists universally and in all processes, whether in the simple or in the complex forms of motion, whether in objective phenomena or ideological phenomena. But does contradiction also exist at the initial stage of each process?

Is there a movement of opposites from beginning to end in the process of development of every single thing?

As can be seen from the articles written by Soviet philosophers criticizing it, the Deborin school maintains that contradiction appears not at the inception of a process but only when it has developed to a certain stage. If this were the case, then the cause of the development of the process before that stage would be external and not internal. Deborin thus reverts to the metaphysical theories of external causality and of mechanism. Applying this view in the analysis of concrete problems, the Deborin school sees only differences but not contradictions between the kulaks and the peasants in general under existing conditions in the Soviet Union, thus entirely agreeing with Bukharin. In analysing the French Revolution, it holds that before the Revolution there were likewise only differences but not contradictions within the Third Estate, which was composed of the workers, the peasants and the bourgeoisie. These views of the Deborin school are anti-Marxist. This school does not understand that each and every difference already contains contradiction and that difference itself is contradiction. Labour and capital have been in contradiction ever since the two classes came into being, only at first the contradiction had not yet become intense. Even under the social conditions existing in the Soviet Union, there is a difference between workers and peasants and this very difference is a contradiction, although, unlike the contradiction between labour and capital, it will not become intensified into antagonism or assume the form of class struggle; the workers and the peasants have established a firm alliance in the course of socialist construction and are gradually resolving this contradiction in the course of the advance from socialism to communism. The question is one of different kinds of contradiction, not of the presence or absence of contradiction. Contradiction is universal and absolute, it is present in the process of development of all things and permeates every process from beginning to end.

What is meant by the emergence of a new process? The old unity with its constituent opposites yields to a new unity with its constituent opposites, whereupon a new process emerges to replace the old. The old process ends and the new one begins. The new process contains new contradictions and begins its own history of the development of contradictions.

As Lenin pointed out, Marx in his *Capital* gave a model analysis of this movement of opposites which runs through the process of development of things from beginning to end. This is the method that must be employed in studying the development of all things. Lenin, too, employed this method correctly and adhered to it in all his writings.

In his *Capital*, Marx first analyses the simplest, most ordinary and fundamental, most common and everyday *relation* of bourgeois (commodity) society, a relation encountered billions of times, viz. the exchange of commodities. In this very simple phenomenon (in this "cell" of bourgeois society) analysis reveals *all* the contradictions (or the germs of *all* the contradictions) of modern society. The subsequent exposition shows us the development (*both* growth *and* movement) of these contradictions and of this society in the Σ [summation] of its individual parts, from its beginning to its end.

Lenin added, "Such must also be the method of exposition (or study) of dialectics in general."[9]

Chinese Communists must learn this method; only then will they be able correctly to analyse the history and the present state of the Chinese revolution and infer its future.

III. THE PARTICULARITY OF CONTRADICTION

Contradiction is present in the process of development of all things; it permeates the process of development of each thing from beginning to end. This is the universality and absoluteness of contradiction which we have discussed above. Now let us discuss the particularity and relativity of contradiction.

This problem should be studied on several levels.

First, the contradiction in each form of motion of matter has its particularity. Man's knowledge of matter is knowledge of its forms of motion, because there is nothing in this world except matter in motion and this motion must assume certain forms. In considering each form of motion of matter, we must observe the points which it has in common with other forms of motion. But what is especially important and necessary, constituting as it does the foundation of our knowledge of a thing, is to observe what is particular to this form of motion of matter, namely, to observe the qualitative difference

37

between this form of motion and other forms. Only when we have done so can we distinguish between things. Every form of motion contains within itself its own particular contradiction. This particular contradiction constitutes the particular essence which distinguishes one thing from another. It is the internal cause or, as it may be called, the basis for the immense variety of things in the world. There are many forms of motion in nature, mechanical motion, sound, light, heat, electricity, dissociation, combination, and so on. All these forms are interdependent, but in its essence each is different from the others. The particular essence of each form of motion is determined by its own particular contradiction. This holds true not only for nature but also for social and ideological phenomena. Every form of society, every form of ideology, has its own particular contradiction and particular essence.

The sciences are differentiated precisely on the basis of the particular contradictions inherent in their respective objects of study. Thus the contradiction peculiar to a certain field of phenomena constitutes the object of study for a specific branch of science. For example, positive and negative numbers in mathematics; action and reaction in mechanics; positive and negative electricity in physics; dissociation and combination in chemistry; forces of production and relations of production, classes and class struggle, in social science; offence and defence in military science; idealism and materialism, the metaphysical outlook and the dialectical outlook, in philosophy; and so on — all these are the objects of study of different branches of science precisely because each branch has its own particular contradiction and particular essence. Of course, unless we understand the universality of contradiction, we have no way of discovering the universal cause or universal basis for the movement or development of things; however, unless we study the particularity of contradiction, we have no way of determining the particular essence of a thing which differentiates it from other things, no way of discovering the particular cause or particular basis for the movement or development of a thing, and no way of distinguishing one thing from another or of demarcating the fields of science.

As regards the sequence in the movement of man's knowledge, there is always a gradual growth from the knowledge of individual and particular things to the knowledge of things in general. Only after man knows the particular essence of many different things can he proceed to generalization and know the common essence of things.

When man attains the knowledge of this common essence, he uses it as a guide and proceeds to study various concrete things which have not yet been studied, or studied thoroughly, and to discover the particular essence of each; only thus is he able to supplement, enrich and develop his knowledge of their common essence and prevent such knowledge from withering or petrifying. These are the two processes of cognition: one, from the particular to the general, and the other, from the general to the particular. Thus cognition always moves in cycles and (so long as scientific method is strictly adhered to) each cycle advances human knowledge a step higher and so makes it more and more profound. Where our dogmatists err on this question is that, on the one hand, they do not understand that we have to study the particularity of contradiction and know the particular essence of individual things before we can adequately know the universality of contradiction and the common essence of things, and that, on the other hand, they do not understand that after knowing the common essence of things, we must go further and study the concrete things that have not yet been thoroughly studied or have only just emerged. Our dogmatists are lazy-bones. They refuse to undertake any painstaking study of concrete things, they regard general truths as emerging out of the void, they turn them into purely abstract unfathomable formulas, and thereby completely deny and reverse the normal sequence by which man comes to know truth. Nor do they understand the interconnection of the two processes in cognition — from the particular to the general and then from the general to the particular. They understand nothing of the Marxist theory of knowledge.

It is necessary not only to study the particular contradiction and the essence determined thereby of every great system of the forms of motion of matter, but also to study the particular contradiction and the essence of each process in the long course of development of each form of motion of matter. In every form of motion, each process of development which is real (and not imaginary) is qualitatively different. Our study must emphasize and start from this point.

Qualitatively different contradictions can only be resolved by qualitatively different methods. For instance, the contradiction between the proletariat and the bourgeoisie is resolved by the method of socialist revolution; the contradiction between the great masses of the people and the feudal system is resolved by the method of democratic revolution; the contradiction between the colonies and imperialism is resolved by the method of national revolutionary war; the contradiction between the working class and the peasant class in socialist society is resolved by the method of collectivization and mechanization in agriculture; contradiction within the Communist Party is resolved by the method of criticism and self-criticism; the contradiction between society and nature is resolved by the method of developing the productive forces. Processes change, old processes and old contradictions disappear, new processes and new contradictions emerge, and the methods of resolving contradictions differ accordingly. In Russia, there was a fundamental difference between the contradiction resolved by the February Revolution and the contradiction resolved by the October Revolution, as well as between the methods used to resolve them. The principle of using different methods to resolve different contradictions is one which Marxist-Leninists must strictly observe. The dogmatists do not observe this principle; they do not understand that conditions differ in different kinds of revolution and so do not understand that different methods should be used to resolve different contradictions; on the contrary, they invariably adopt what they imagine to be an unalterable formula and arbitrarily apply it everywhere, which only causes setbacks to the revolution or makes a sorry mess of what was originally well done.

In order to reveal the particularity of the contradictions in any process in the development of a thing, in their totality or interconnections, that is, in order to reveal the essence of the process, it is necessary to reveal the particularity of the two aspects of each of the contradictions in that process; otherwise it will be impossible to discover the essence of the process. This likewise requires the utmost attention in our study.

There are many contradictions in the course of development of any major thing. For instance, in the course of China's bourgeois-democratic revolution, where the conditions are exceedingly complex, there exist the contradiction between all the oppressed classes in Chinese society and imperialism, the contradiction between the great masses of the people and feudalism, the contradiction between the proletariat and the bourgeoisie, the contradiction between the peasantry and the urban petty bourgeoisie on the one hand and the bourgeoisie on the other, the contradiction between the various reactionary ruling groups, and so on. These contradictions cannot be treated in the same way since each has its own particularity; moreover, the two aspects of each contradiction cannot be treated in the same way since

40

each aspect has its own characteristics. We who are engaged in the Chinese revolution should not only understand the particularity of these contradictions in their totality, that is, in their interconnections, but should also study the two aspects of each contradiction as the only means of understanding the totality. When we speak of understanding each aspect of a contradiction, we mean understanding what specific position each aspect occupies, what concrete forms it assumes in its interdependence and in its contradiction with its opposite, and what concrete methods are employed in the struggle with its opposite, when the two are both interdependent and in contradiction, and also after the interdependence breaks down. It is of great importance to study these problems. Lenin meant just this when he said that the most essential thing in Marxism, the living soul of Marxism, is the concrete analysis of concrete conditions.[10] Our dogmatists have violated Lenin's teachings; they never use their brains to analyse anything concretely, and in their writings and speeches they always use stereotypes devoid of content, thereby creating a very bad style of work in our Party.

In studying a problem, we must shun subjectivity, one-sidedness and superficiality. To be subjective means not to look at problems objectively, that is, not to use the materialist viewpoint in looking at problems. I have discussed this in my essay "On Practice". To be one-sided means not to look at problems all-sidedly, for example, to understand only China but not Japan, only the Communist Party but not the Kuomintang, only the proletariat but not the bourgeoisie, only the peasants but not the landlords, only the favourable conditions but not the difficult ones, only the past but not the future, only individual parts but not the whole, only the defects but not the achievements, only the plaintiff's case but not the defendant's, only underground revolutionary work but not open revolutionary work, and so on. In a word, it means not to understand the characteristics of both aspects of a contradiction. This is what we mean by looking at a problem one-sidedly. Or it may be called seeing the part but not the whole, seeing the trees but not the forest. That way it is impossible to find the method for resolving a contradiction, it is impossible to accomplish the tasks of the revolution, to carry out assignments well or to develop inner-Party ideological struggle correctly. When Sun Wu Tzu said in discussing military science, "Know the enemy and know yourself, and you can fight a hundred battles with no danger of defeat",[11] he was referring to the two sides in a battle. Wei Cheng[12] of the Tang Dynasty also understood the error of one-sidedness when he said, "Listen to both sides and you will be enlightened, heed only one side and you will be benighted." But our comrades often look at problems one-sidedly, and so they often run into snags. In the novel *Shui Hu Chuan*, Sung Chiang thrice attacked Chu Village.[13] Twice he was defeated because he was ignorant of the local conditions and used the wrong method. Later he changed his method; first he investigated the situation, and he familiarized himself with the maze of roads, then he broke up the alliance between the Li, Hu and Chu Villages and sent his men in disguise into the enemy camp to lie in wait, using a stratagem similar to that of the Trojan Horse in the foreign story. And on the third occasion he won. There are many examples of materialist dialectics in *Shui Hu Chuan*, of which the episode of the three attacks on Chu Village is one of the best. Lenin said:

> . . . in order really to know an object we must embrace, study, all its sides, all connections and "mediations". We shall never achieve this completely, but the demand for all-sidedness is a safeguard against mistakes and rigidity.[14]

We should remember his words. To be superficial means to consider neither the characteristics of a contradiction in its totality nor the characteristics of each of its aspects; it means to deny the necessity for probing deeply into a thing and minutely studying the characteristics of its contradiction, but instead merely to look from afar and, after glimpsing the rough outline, immediately to try to resolve the contradiction (to answer a question, settle a dispute, handle work, or direct a military operation). This way of doing things is bound to lead to trouble. The reason the dogmatist and empiricist comrades in China have made mistakes lies precisely in their subjectivist, one-sided and superficial way of looking at things. To be one-sided and superficial is at the same time to be subjective. For all objective things are actually interconnected and are governed by inner laws, but instead of undertaking the task of reflecting things as they really are some people only look at things one-sidedly or superficially and who know neither their interconnections nor their inner laws, and so their method is subjectivist.

Not only does the whole process of the movement of opposites in the development of a thing, both in their interconnections and in

42

each of the aspects, have particular features to which we must give attention, but each stage in the process has its particular features to which we must give attention too.

The fundamental contradiction in the process of development of a thing and the essence of the process determined by this fundamental contradiction will not disappear until the process is completed; but in a lengthy process the conditions usually differ at each stage. The reason is that, although the nature of the fundamental contradiction in the process of development of a thing and the essence of the process remain unchanged, the fundamental contradiction becomes more and more intensified as it passes from one stage to another in the lengthy process. In addition, among the numerous major and minor contradictions which are determined or influenced by the fundamental contradiction, some become intensified, some are temporarily or partially resolved or mitigated, and some new ones emerge; hence the process is marked by stages. If people do not pay attention to the stages in the process of development of a thing, they cannot deal with its contradictions properly.

For instance, when the capitalism of the era of free competition developed into imperialism, there was no change in the class nature of the two classes in fundamental contradiction, namely, the proletariat and the bourgeoisie, or in the capitalist essence of society; however, the contradiction between these two classes became intensified, the contradiction between monopoly and non-monopoly capital emerged, the contradiction between the colonial powers and the colonies became intensified, the contradiction among the capitalist countries resulting from their uneven development manifested itself with particular sharpness, and thus there arose the special stage of capitalism, the stage of imperialism. Leninism is the Marxism of the era of imperialism and proletarian revolution precisely because Lenin and Stalin have correctly explained these contradictions and correctly formulated the theory and tactics of the proletarian revolution for their resolution.

Take the process of China's bourgeois-democratic revolution, which began with the Revolution of 1911; it, too, has several distinct stages. In particular, the revolution in its period of bourgeois leadership and the revolution in its period of proletarian leadership represent two vastly different historical stages. In other words, proletarian leadership has fundamentally changed the whole face of the revolution, has brought about a new alignment of classes, given rise to a tremendous upsurge in the peasant revolution, imparted thoroughness to the revolution against imperialism and feudalism, created the possibility of the transition from the democratic revolution to the socialist revolution, and so on. None of these was possible in the period when the revolution was under bourgeois leadership. Although no change has taken place in the nature of the fundamental contradiction in the process as a whole, *i.e.*, in the anti-imperialist, anti-feudal, democratic-revolutionary nature of the process (the opposite of which is its semi-colonial and semi-feudal nature), nonetheless this process has passed through several stages of development in the course of more than twenty years; during this time many great events have taken place — the failure of the Revolution of 1911 and the establishment of the regime of the Northern warlords, the formation of the first national united front and the revolution of 1924-27, the break-up of the united front and the desertion of the bourgeoisie to the side of the counter-revolution, the wars among the new warlords, the Agrarian Revolutionary War, the establishment of the second national united front and the War of Resistance Against Japan. These stages are marked by particular features such as the intensification of certain contradictions (*e.g.*, the Agrarian Revolutionary War and the Japanese invasion of the four northeastern provinces), the partial or temporary resolution of other contradictions (*e.g.*, the destruction of the Northern warlords and our confiscation of the land of the landlords), and the emergence of yet other contradictions (*e.g.*, the conflicts among the new warlords, and the landlords' recapture of the land after the loss of our revolutionary base areas in the south).

In studying the particularities of the contradictions at each stage in the process of development of a thing, we must not only observe them in their interconnections or their totality, we must also examine the two aspects of each contradiction.

For instance, consider the Kuomintang and the Communist Party. Take one aspect, the Kuomintang. In the period of the first united front, the Kuomintang carried out Sun Yat-sen's Three Great Policies of alliance with Russia, co-operation with the Communist Party, and assistance to the peasants and workers; hence it was revolutionary and vigorous, it was an alliance of various classes for the democratic revolution. After 1927, however, the Kuomintang changed into its opposite and became a reactionary bloc of the landlords and big

44

bourgeoisie. After the Sian Incident in December 1936, it began another change in the direction of ending the civil war and co-operating with the Communist Party for joint opposition to Japanese imperialism. Such have been the particular features of the Kuomintang in the three stages. Of course, these features have arisen from a variety of causes. Now take the other aspect, the Chinese Communist Party. In the period of the first united front, the Chinese Communist Party was in its infancy; it courageously led the revolution of 1924-27 but revealed its immaturity in its understanding of the character, the tasks and the methods of the revolution, and consequently it became possible for Chen Tu-hsiuism, which appeared during the latter part of this revolution, to assert itself and bring about the defeat of the revolution. After 1927, the Communist Party courageously led the Agrarian Revolutionary War and created the revolutionary army and revolutionary base areas; however, it committed adventurist errors which brought about very great losses both to the army and to the base areas. Since 1935 the Party has corrected these errors and has been leading the new united front for resistance to Japan; this great struggle is now developing. At the present stage, the Communist Party is a Party that has gone through the test of two revolutions and acquired a wealth of experience. Such have been the particular features of the Chinese Communist Party in the three stages. These features, too, have arisen from a variety of causes. Without studying both these sets of features we cannot understand the particular relations between the two parties during the various stages of their development, namely, the establishment of a united front, the break-up of the united front, and the establishment of another united front. What is even more fundamental for the study of the particular features of the two parties is the examination of the class basis of the two parties and the resultant contradictions which have arisen between each party and other forces at different periods. For instance, in the period of its first co-operation with the Communist Party, the Kuomintang stood in contradiction to foreign imperialism and was therefore anti-imperialist; on the other hand, it stood in contradiction to the great masses of the people within the country — although in words it promised many benefits to the working people, in fact it gave them little or nothing. In the period when it carried on the anti-Communist war, the Kuomintang collaborated with imperialism and feudalism against the great masses of the people and wiped out all the gains they had won

45

in the revolution, and thereby intensified its contradictions with them. In the present period of the anti-Japanese war, the Kuomintang stands in contradiction to Japanese imperialism and wants co-operation with the Communist Party, without however relaxing its struggle against the Communist Party and the people or its oppression of them. As for the Communist Party, it has always, in every period, stood with the great masses of the people against imperialism and feudalism, but in the present period of the anti-Japanese war, it has adopted a moderate policy towards the Kuomintang and the domestic feudal forces because the Kuomintang has expressed itself in favour of resisting Japan. The above circumstances have resulted now in alliance between the two parties and now in struggle between them, and even during the periods of alliance there has been a complicated state of simultaneous alliance and struggle. If we do not study the particular features of both aspects of the contradiction, we shall fail to understand not only the relations of each party with the other forces, but also the relations between the two parties.

It can thus be seen that in studying the particularity of any kind of contradiction — the contradiction in each form of motion of matter, the contradiction in each of its processes of development, the two aspects of the contradiction in each process, the contradiction at each stage of a process, and the two aspects of the contradiction at each stage — in studying the particularity of all these contradictions, we must not be subjective and arbitrary but must analyse it concretely. Without concrete analysis there can be no knowledge of the particularity of any contradiction. We must always remember Lenin's words, the concrete analysis of concrete conditions.

Marx and Engels were the first to provide us with excellent models of such concrete analysis.

When Marx and Engels applied the law of contradiction in things to the study of the socio-historical process, they discovered the contradiction between the productive forces and the relations of production, they discovered the contradiction between the exploiting and exploited classes and also the resultant contradiction between the economic base and its superstructure (politics, ideology, etc.), and they discovered how these contradictions inevitably lead to different kinds of social revolution in different kinds of class society.

When Marx applied this law to the study of the economic structure of capitalist society, he discovered that the basic contradiction of this society is the contradiction between the social character of production and the private character of ownership. This contradiction manifests itself in the contradiction between the organized character of production in individual enterprises and the anarchic character of production in society as a whole. In terms of class relations, it manifests itself in the contradiction between the bourgeoisie and the proletariat.

Because the range of things is vast and there is no limit to their development, what is universal in one context becomes particular in another. Conversely, what is particular in one context becomes universal in another. The contradiction in the capitalist system between the social character of production and the private ownership of the means of production is common to all countries where capitalism exists and develops; as far as capitalism is concerned, this constitutes the universality of contradiction. But this contradiction of capitalism belongs only to a certain historical stage in the general development of class society; as far as the contradiction between the productive forces and the relations of production in class society as a whole is concerned, it constitutes the particularity of contradiction. However, in the course of dissecting the particularity of all these contradictions in capitalist society, Marx gave a still more profound, more adequate and more complete elucidation of the universality of the contradiction between the productive forces and the relations of production in class society in general.

Since the particular is united with the universal and since the universality as well as the particularity of contradiction is inherent in everything, universality residing in particularity, we should, when studying an object, try to discover both the particular and the universal and their interconnection, to discover both particularity and universality and also their interconnection within the object itself, and to discover the interconnections of this object with the many objects outside it. When Stalin explained the historical roots of Leninism in his famous work, *The Foundations of Leninism,* he analysed the international situation in which Leninism arose, analysed those contradictions of capitalism which reached their culmination under imperialism, and showed how these contradictions made proletarian revolution a matter for immediate action and created favourable conditions for a direct onslaught on capitalism. What is more, he analysed the reasons why Russia became the cradle of Leninism, why

47

tsarist Russia became the focus of all the contradictions of imperialism, and why it was possible for the Russian proletariat to become the vanguard of the international revolutionary proletariat. Thus, Stalin analysed the universality of contradiction in imperialism, showing why Leninism is the Marxism of the era of imperialism and proletarian revolution, and at the same time analysed the particularity of tsarist Russian imperialism within this general contradiction, showing why Russia became the birthplace of the theory and tactics of proletarian revolution and how the universality of contradiction is contained in this particularity. Stalin's analysis provides us with a model for understanding the particularity and the universality of contradiction and their interconnection.

On the question of using dialectics in the study of objective phenomena, Marx and Engels, and likewise Lenin and Stalin, always enjoin people not to be in any way subjective and arbitrary but, from the concrete conditions in the actual objective movement of these phenomena, to discover their concrete contradictions, the concrete position of each aspect of every contradiction and the concrete interrelations of the contradictions. Our dogmatists do not have this attitude in study and therefore can never get anything right. We must take warning from their failure and learn to acquire this attitude, which is the only correct one in study.

The relationship between the universality and the particularity of contradiction is the relationship between the general character and the individual character of contradiction. By the former we mean that contradiction exists in and runs through all processes from beginning to end; motion, things, processes, thinking — all are contradictions. To deny contradiction is to deny everything. This is a universal truth for all times and all countries, which admits of no exception. Hence the general character, the absoluteness of contradiction. But this general character is contained in every individual character; without individual character there can be no general character. If all individual character were removed, what general character would remain? It is because each contradiction is particular that individual character arises. All individual character exists conditionally and temporarily, and hence is relative.

This truth concerning general and individual character, concerning absoluteness and relativity, is the quintessence of the problem of contradiction in things; failure to understand it is tantamount to abandoning dialectics.

IV. THE PRINCIPAL CONTRADICTION AND THE PRINCIPAL ASPECT OF A CONTRADICTION

There are still two points in the problem of the particularity of contradiction which must be singled out for analysis, namely, the principal contradiction and the principal aspect of a contradiction.

There are many contradictions in the process of development of a complex thing, and one of them is necessarily the principal contradiction whose existence and development determine or influence the existence and development of the other contradictions.

For instance, in capitalist society the two forces in contradiction, the proletariat and the bourgeoisie, form the principal contradiction. The other contradictions, such as those between the remnant feudal class and the bourgeoisie, between the peasant petty bourgeoisie and the bourgeoisie, between the proletariat and the peasant petty bourgeoisie, between the non-monopoly capitalists and the monopoly capitalists, between bourgeois democracy and bourgeois fascism, among the capitalist countries and between imperialism and the colonies, are all determined or influenced by this principal contradiction.

In a semi-colonial country such as China, the relationship between the principal contradiction and the non-principal contradictions presents a complicated picture.

When imperialism launches a war of aggression against such a country, all its various classes, except for some traitors, can temporarily unite in a national war against imperialism. At such a time, the contradiction between imperialism and the country concerned becomes the principal contradiction, while all the contradictions among the various classes within the country (including what was the principal contradiction, between the feudal system and the great masses of the people) are temporarily relegated to a secondary and subordinate position. So it was in China in the Opium War of 1840, the Sino-Japanese War of 1894 and the Yi Ho Tuan War of 1900, and so it is now in the present Sino-Japanese War.

But in another situation, the contradictions change position. When imperialism carries on its oppression not by war, but by milder means — political, economic and cultural — the ruling classes in semi-colonial countries capitulate to imperialism, and the two form an alliance for the joint oppression of the masses of the people. At such a time, the masses often resort to civil war against the alliance of imperialism and the feudal classes, while imperialism often employs indirect methods rather than direct action in helping the reactionaries in the semi-colonial countries to oppress the people, and thus the internal contradictions become particularly sharp. This is what happened in China in the Revolutionary War of 1911, the Revolutionary War of 1924-27, and the ten years of Agrarian Revolutionary War after 1927. Wars among the various reactionary ruling groups in the semi-colonial countries, *e.g.*, the wars among the warlords in China, fall into the same category.

When a revolutionary civil war develops to the point of threatening the very existence of imperialism and its running dogs, the domestic reactionaries, imperialism often adopts other methods in order to maintain its rule; it either tries to split the revolutionary front from within or sends armed forces to help the domestic reactionaries directly. At such a time, foreign imperialism and domestic reaction stand quite openly at one pole while the masses of the people stand at the other pole, thus forming the principal contradiction which determines or influences the development of the other contradictions. The assistance given by various capitalist countries to the Russian reactionaries after the October Revolution is an example of armed intervention. Chiang Kai-shek's betrayal in 1927 is an example of splitting the revolutionary front.

But whatever happens, there is no doubt at all that at every stage in the development of a process, there is only one principal contradiction which plays the leading role.

Hence, if in any process there are a number of contradictions, one of them must be the principal contradiction playing the leading and decisive role, while the rest occupy a secondary and subordinate position. Therefore, in studying any complex process in which there are two or more contradictions, we must devote every effort to finding its principal contradiction. Once this principal contradiction is grasped, all problems can be readily solved. This is the method Marx taught us in his study of capitalist society. Likewise Lenin and Stalin taught us this method when they studied imperialism and the general crisis of capitalism and when they studied the Soviet economy. There are thousands of scholars and men of action who do not understand it, and the result is that, lost in a fog, they are unable to get to the heart of a problem and naturally cannot find a way to resolve its contradictions.

50

As we have said, one must not treat all the contradictions in a process as being equal but must distinguish between the principal and the secondary contradictions, and pay special attention to grasping the principal one. But, in any given contradiction, whether principal or secondary, should the two contradictory aspects be treated as equal? Again, no. In any contradiction the development of the contradictory aspects is uneven. Sometimes they seem to be in equilibrium, which is however only temporary and relative, while unevenness is basic. Of the two contradictory aspects, one must be principal and the other secondary. The principal aspect is the one playing the leading role in the contradiction. The nature of a thing is determined mainly by the principal aspect of a contradiction, the aspect which has gained the dominant position.

But this situation is not static; the principal and the non-principal aspects of a contradiction transform themselves into each other and the nature of the thing changes accordingly. In a given process or at a given stage in the development of a contradiction, A is the principal aspect and B is the non-principal aspect; at another stage or in another process the roles are reversed — a change determined by the extent of the increase or decrease in the force of each aspect in its struggle against the other in the course of the development of a thing.

We often speak of "the new superseding the old". The supersession of the old by the new is a general, eternal and inviolable law of the universe. The transformation of one thing into another, through leaps of different forms in accordance with its essence and external conditions — this is the process of the new superseding the old. In each thing there is contradiction between its new and its old aspects, and this gives rise to a series of struggles with many twists and turns. As a result of these struggles, the new aspect changes from being minor to being major and rises to predominance, while the old aspect changes from being major to being minor and gradually dies out. And the moment the new aspect gains dominance over the old, the old thing changes qualitatively into a new thing. It can thus be seen that the nature of a thing is mainly determined by the principal aspect of the contradiction, the aspect which has gained predominance. When the principal aspect which has gained predominance changes, the nature of a thing changes accordingly.

In capitalist society, capitalism has changed its position from being a subordinate force in the old feudal era to being the dominant force, and the nature of society has accordingly changed from feudal

51

to capitalist. In the new, capitalist era, the feudal forces changed from their former dominant position to a subordinate one, gradually dying out. Such was the case, for example, in Britain and France. With the development of the productive forces, the bourgeoisie changes from being a new class playing a progressive role to being an old class playing a reactionary role, until it is finally overthrown by the proletariat and becomes a class deprived of privately owned means of production and stripped of power, when it, too, gradually dies out. The proletariat, which is much more numerous than the bourgeoisie and grows simultaneously with it but under its rule, is a new force which, initially subordinate to the bourgeoisie, gradually gains strength, becomes an independent class playing the leading role in history, and finally seizes political power and becomes the ruling class. Thereupon the nature of society changes and the old capitalist society becomes the new socialist society. This is the path already taken by the Soviet Union, a path that all other countries will inevitably take.

Look at China, for instance. Imperialism occupies the principal position in the contradiction in which China has been reduced to a semi-colony, it oppresses the Chinese people, and China has been changed from an independent country into a semi-colonial one. But this state of affairs will inevitably change; in the struggle between the two sides, the power of the Chinese people which is growing under the leadership of the proletariat will inevitably change China from a semi-colony into an independent country, whereas imperialism will be overthrown and old China will inevitably change into New China.

The change of old China into New China also involves a change in the relation between the old feudal forces and the new popular forces within the country. The old feudal landlord class will be overthrown, and from being the ruler it will change into being the ruled; and this class, too, will gradually die out. From being the ruled the people, led by the proletariat, will become the rulers. Thereupon, the nature of Chinese society will change and the old, semi-colonial and semi-feudal society will change into a new democratic society.

Instances of such reciprocal transformation are found in our past experience. The Ching Dynasty which ruled China for nearly three hundred years was overthrown in the Revolution of 1911, and the revolutionary *Tung Meng Hui* under Sun Yat-sen's leadership was victorious for a time. In the Revolutionary War of 1924-27, the revolutionary forces of the Communist-Kuomintang alliance in the south changed from being weak to being strong and won victory in the Northern Expedition, while the Northern warlords who once ruled the roost were overthrown. In 1927, the people's forces led by the Communist Party were greatly reduced numerically under the attacks of Kuomintang reaction, but with the elimination of opportunism within their ranks they gradually grew again. In the revolutionary base areas under Communist leadership, the peasants have been transformed from being the ruled to being the rulers, while the land-lords have undergone a reverse transformation. It is always so in the world, the new displacing the old, the old being superseded by the new, the old being eliminated to make way for the new, and the new emerging out of the old.

At certain times in the revolutionary struggle, the difficulties out-weigh the favourable conditions and so constitute the principal aspect of the contradiction and the favourable conditions constitute the secondary aspect. But through their efforts the revolutionaries can overcome the difficulties step by step and open up a favourable new situation; thus a difficult situation yields place to a favourable one. This is what happened after the failure of the revolution in China in 1927 and during the Long March of the Chinese Red Army. In the present Sino-Japanese War, China is again in a difficult position, but we can change this and fundamentally transform the situation as between China and Japan. Conversely, favourable conditions can be transformed into difficulty if the revolutionaries make mistakes. Thus the victory of the revolution of 1924-27 turned into defeat. The revolutionary base areas which grew up in the southern provinces after 1927 had all suffered defeat by 1934.

When we engage in study, the same holds good for the con-tradiction in the passage from ignorance to knowledge. At the very beginning of our study of Marxism, our ignorance of or scanty ac-quaintance with Marxism stands in contradiction to knowledge of Marxism. But by assiduous study, ignorance can be transformed into knowledge, scanty knowledge into substantial knowledge, and blind-ness in the application of Marxism into mastery of its application.

Some people think that this is not true of certain contradictions. For instance, in the contradiction between the productive forces and the relations of production, the productive forces are the principal aspect; in the contradiction between theory and practice, practice is the principal aspect; in the contradiction between the economic base and the superstructure, the economic base is the principal aspect;

and there is no change in their respective positions. This is the mechanical materialist conception, not the dialectical materialist conception. True, the productive forces, practice and the economic base generally play the principal and decisive role; whoever denies this is not a materialist. But it must also be admitted that in certain conditions, such aspects as the relations of production, theory and the superstructure in turn manifest themselves in the principal and decisive role. When it is impossible for the productive forces to develop without a change in the relations of production, then the change in the relations of production plays the principal and decisive role. The creation and advocacy of revolutionary theory plays the principal and decisive role in those times of which Lenin said, "Without revolutionary theory there can be no revolutionary movement."[15] When a task, no matter which, has to be performed, but there is as yet no guiding line, method, plan or policy, the principal and decisive thing is to decide on a guiding line, method, plan or policy. When the superstructure (politics, culture, etc.) obstructs the development of the economic base, political and cultural changes become principal and decisive. Are we going against materialism when we say this? No. The reason is that while we recognize that in the general development of history the material determines the mental and social being determines social consciousness, we also — and indeed must — recognize the reaction of mental on material things, of social consciousness on social being and of the superstructure on the economic base. This does not go against materialism; on the contrary, it avoids mechanical materialism and firmly upholds dialectical materialism.

In studying the particularity of contradiction, unless we examine these two facets — the principal and the non-principal contradictions in a process, and the principal and the non-principal aspects of a contradiction — that is, unless we examine the distinctive character of these two facets of contradiction, we shall get bogged down in abstractions, be unable to understand contradiction concretely and consequently be unable to find the correct method of resolving it. The distinctive character or particularity of these two facets of contradiction represents the unevenness of the forces that are in contradiction. Nothing in this world develops absolutely evenly; we must oppose the theory of even development or the theory of equilibrium. Moreover, it is these concrete features of a contradiction and the changes in the principal and non-principal aspects of a contradiction in the course of its development that manifest the force of the new superseding the old. The study of the various states of unevenness in contradictions, of the principal and non-principal contradictions and of the principal and the non-principal aspects of a contradiction constitutes an essential method by which a revolutionary political party correctly determines its strategic and tactical policies both in political and in military affairs. All Communists must give it attention.

V. THE IDENTITY AND STRUGGLE OF THE ASPECTS OF A CONTRADICTION

When we understand the universality and the particularity of contradiction, we must proceed to study the problem of the identity and struggle of the aspects of a contradiction.

Identity, unity, coincidence, interpenetration, interpermeation, interdependence (or mutual dependence for existence), interconnection or mutual co-operation — all these different terms mean the same thing and refer to the following two points: first, the existence of each of the two aspects of a contradiction in the process of the development of a thing presupposes the existence of the other aspect, and both aspects coexist in a single entity; second, in given conditions, each of the two contradictory aspects transforms itself into its opposite. This is the meaning of identity.

Lenin said:

> *Dialectics* is the teaching which shows how *opposites* can be and how they happen to be (how they become) *identical* — under what conditions they are identical, transforming themselves into one another, — why the human mind should take these opposites not as dead, rigid, but as living, conditional, mobile, transforming themselves into one another.[16]

What does this passage mean?

The contradictory aspects in every process exclude each other, struggle with each other and are in opposition to each other. Without exception, they are contained in the process of development of all things and in all human thought. A simple process contains only a single pair of opposites, while a complex process contains more. And in turn, the pairs of opposites are in contradiction to one another.

55

That is how all things in the objective world and all human thought are constituted and how they are set in motion.

This being so, there is an utter lack of identity or unity. How then can one speak of identity or unity?

The fact is that no contradictory aspect can exist in isolation. Without its opposite aspect, each loses the condition for its existence. Just think, can any one contradictory aspect of a thing or of a concept in the human mind exist independently? Without life, there would be no death; without death, there would be no life. Without "above", there would be no "below"; without "below", there would be no "above". Without misfortune, there would be no good fortune; without good fortune, there would be no misfortune. Without facility, there would be no difficulty; without difficulty, there would be no facility. Without landlords, there would be no tenant-peasants; without tenant-peasants, there would be no landlords. Without the bourgeoisie, there would be no proletariat; without the proletariat, there would be no bourgeoisie. Without imperialist oppression of nations, there would be no colonies or semi-colonies; without colonies or semi-colonies, there would be no imperialist oppression of nations. It is so with all opposites; in given conditions, on the one hand they are opposed to each other, and on the other they are interconnected, interpenetrating, interpermeating and interdependent, and this character is described as identity. In given conditions, all contradictory aspects possess the character of non-identity and hence are described as being in contradiction. But they also possess the character of identity and hence are interconnected. This is what Lenin means when he says that dialectics studies "how *opposites* can be . . . *identical*". How then can they be identical? Because each is the condition for the other's existence. This is the first meaning of identity.

But is it enough to say merely that each of the contradictory aspects is the condition for the other's existence, that there is identity between them and that consequently they can coexist in a single entity? No, it is not. The matter does not end with their dependence on each other for their existence; what is more important is their transformation into each other. That is to say, in given conditions, each of the contradictory aspects within a thing transforms itself into its opposite, changes its position to that of its opposite. This is the second meaning of the identity of contradiction.

Why is there identity here, too? You see, by means of revolution the proletariat, at one time the ruled, is transformed into the ruler, while the bourgeoisie, the erstwhile ruler, is transformed into the ruled and changes its position to that originally occupied by its opposite. This has already taken place in the Soviet Union, as it will take place throughout the world. If there were no interconnection and identity of opposites in given conditions, how could such a change take place?

The Kuomintang, which played a certain positive role at a certain stage in modern Chinese history, became a counter-revolutionary party after 1927 because of its inherent class nature and because of imperialist blandishments (these being the conditions); but it has been compelled to agree to resist Japan because of the sharpening of the contradiction between China and Japan and because of the Communist Party's policy of the united front (these being the conditions). Things in contradiction change into one another, and herein lies a definite identity.

Our agrarian revolution has been a process in which the landlord class owning the land is transformed into a class that has lost its land, while the peasants who once lost their land are transformed into small holders who have acquired land, and it will be such a process once again. In given conditions having and not having, acquiring and losing, are interconnected; there is identity of the two sides. Under socialism, private peasant ownership is transformed into the public ownership of socialist agriculture; this has already taken place in the Soviet Union, as it will take place everywhere else. There is a bridge leading from private property to public property, which in philosophy is called identity, or transformation into each other, or interpenetration.

To consolidate the dictatorship of the proletariat or the dictatorship of the people is in fact to prepare the conditions for abolishing this dictatorship and advancing to the higher stage when all state systems are eliminated. To establish and build the Communist Party is in fact to prepare the conditions for the elimination of the Communist Party and all political parties. To build a revolutionary army under the leadership of the Communist Party and to carry on revolutionary war is in fact to prepare the conditions for the permanent elimination of war. These opposites are at the same time complementary.

War and peace, as everybody knows, transform themselves into each other. War is transformed into peace; for instance, the First World War was transformed into the post-war peace, and the civil war in China has now stopped, giving place to internal peace. Peace

57

is transformed into war; for instance, the Kuomintang-Communist co-operation was transformed into war in 1927, and today's situation of world peace may be transformed into a second world war. Why is this so? Because in class society such contradictory things as war and peace have an identity in given conditions.

All contradictory things are interconnected; not only do they coexist in a single entity in given conditions, but in other given conditions, they also transform themselves into each other. This is the full meaning of the identity of opposites. This is what Lenin meant when he discussed "how they happen to be (how they become) *identical* — under what conditions they are identical, transforming themselves into one another".

Why is it that "the human mind should take these opposites not as dead, rigid, but as living, conditional, mobile, transforming themselves into one another"? Because that is just how things are in objective reality. The fact is that the unity or identity of opposites in objective things is not dead or rigid, but is living, conditional, mobile, temporary and relative; in given conditions, every contradictory aspect transforms itself into its opposite. Reflected in man's thinking, this becomes the Marxist world outlook of materialist dialectics. It is only the reactionary ruling classes of the past and present and the metaphysicians in their service who regard opposites not as living, conditional, mobile and transforming themselves into one another, but as dead and rigid, and they propagate this fallacy everywhere to delude the masses of the people, thus seeking to perpetuate their rule. The task of Communists is to expose the fallacies of the re-actionaries and metaphysicians, to propagate the dialectics inherent in things, and so accelerate the transformation of things and achieve the goal of revolution.

In speaking of the identity of opposites in given conditions, what we are referring to is real and concrete opposites and the real and concrete transformations of opposites into one another. There are innumerable transformations in mythology, for instance, Kua Fu's race with the sun in *Shan Hai Ching*,[17] Yi's shooting down of nine suns in *Huai Nan Tzu*,[18] the Monkey King's seventy-two metamorphoses in *Hsi Yu Chi*,[19] the numerous episodes of ghosts and foxes metamorphosed into human beings in the *Strange Tales of Liao Chai*,[20] etc. But these legendary transformations of opposites are not concrete changes reflecting concrete contradictions. They are naive, imaginary, subjectively conceived transformations conjured up in men's minds by innumerable real and complex transformations of opposites into one another. Marx said, "All mythology masters and dominates and shapes the forces of nature in and through the imagination; hence it disappears as soon as man gains mastery over the forces of nature."[21] The myriads of changes in mythology (and also in nursery tales) delight people because they imaginatively picture man's conquest of the forces of nature, and the best myths possess "eternal charm", as Marx put it; but myths are not built out of the concrete contradictions existing in given conditions and therefore are not a scientific reflection of reality. That is to say, in myths or nursery tales the aspects constituting a contradiction have only an imaginary identity, not a concrete identity. The scientific reflection of the identity in real transformations is Marxist dialectics.

Why can an egg but not a stone be transformed into a chicken? Why is there identity between war and peace and none between war and a stone? Why can human beings give birth only to human beings and not to anything else? The sole reason is that the identity of opposites exists only in necessary given conditions. Without these necessary given conditions there can be no identity whatsoever.

Why is it that in Russia in 1917 the bourgeois-democratic February Revolution was directly linked with the proletarian socialist October Revolution, while in France the bourgeois revolution was not directly linked with a socialist revolution and the Paris Commune of 1871 ended in failure? Why is it, on the other hand, that the nomadic system of Mongolia and Central Asia has been directly linked with socialism? Why is it that the Chinese revolution can avoid a capitalist future and be directly linked with socialism without taking the old historical road of the Western countries, without passing through a period of bourgeois dictatorship? The sole reason is the concrete conditions of the time. When certain necessary conditions are present, certain contradictions arise in the process of development of things and, moreover, the opposites contained in them are interdependent and become transformed into one another; otherwise none of this would be possible.

Such is the problem of identity. What then is struggle? And what is the relation between identity and struggle?

Lenin said:

> The unity (coincidence, identity, equal action) of opposites is conditional, temporary, transitory, relative. The struggle of

59

mutually exclusive opposites is absolute, just as development and motion are absolute.[22]

What does this passage mean?

All processes have a beginning and an end, all processes transform themselves into their opposites. The constancy of all processes is relative, but the mutability manifested in the transformation of one process into another is absolute.

There are two states of motion in all things, that of relative rest and that of conspicuous change. Both are caused by the struggle between the two contradictory elements contained in a thing. When the thing is in the first state of motion, it is undergoing only quantitative and not qualitative change and consequently presents the outward appearance of being at rest. When the thing is in the second state of motion, the quantitative change of the first state has already reached a culminating point and gives rise to the dissolution of the thing as an entity and thereupon a qualitative change ensues, hence the appearance of a conspicuous change. Such unity, solidarity, combination, harmony, balance, stalemate, deadlock, rest, constancy, equilibrium, solidity, attraction, etc., as we see in daily life, are all the appearances of things in the state of quantitative change. On the other hand, the dissolution of unity, that is, the destruction of this solidarity, combination, harmony, balance, stalemate, deadlock, rest, constancy, equilibrium, solidity and attraction, and the change of each into its opposite are all the appearances of things in the state of qualitative change, the transformation of one process into another. Things are constantly transforming themselves from the first into the second state of motion; the struggle of opposites goes on in both states but the contradiction is resolved through the second state. That is why we say that the unity of opposites is conditional, temporary and relative, while the struggle of mutually exclusive opposites is absolute.

When we said above that two opposite things can coexist in a single entity and can transform themselves into each other because there is identity between them, we were speaking of conditionality, that is to say, in given conditions two contradictory things can be united and can transform themselves into each other, but in the absence of these conditions, they cannot constitute a contradiction, cannot coexist in the same entity and cannot transform themselves into one another. It is because the identity of opposites obtains only in given

60

conditions that we have said identity is conditional and relative. We may add that the struggle between opposites permeates a process from beginning to end and makes one process transform itself into another, that it is ubiquitous, and that struggle is therefore unconditional and absolute.

The combination of conditional, relative identity and unconditional, absolute struggle constitutes the movement of opposites in all things.

We Chinese often say, "Things that oppose each other also complement each other."[23] That is, things opposed to each other have identity. This saying is dialectical and contrary to metaphysics. "Oppose each other" refers to the mutual exclusion or the struggle of two contradictory aspects. "Complement each other" means that in given conditions the two contradictory aspects unite and achieve identity. Yet struggle is inherent in identity and without struggle there can be no identity.

In identity there is struggle, in particularity there is universality, and in individuality there is generality. To quote Lenin, ". . . there *is* an absolute *in* the relative."[24]

VI. THE PLACE OF ANTAGONISM IN CONTRADICTION

The question of the struggle of opposites includes the question of what is antagonism. Our answer is that antagonism is one form, but not the only form, of the struggle of opposites.

In human history, antagonism between classes exists as a particular manifestation of the struggle of opposites. Consider the contradiction between the exploiting and the exploited classes. Such contradictory classes coexist for a long time in the same society, be it slave society, feudal society or capitalist society, and they struggle with each other; but it is not until the contradiction between the two classes develops to a certain stage that it assumes the form of open antagonism and develops into revolution. The same holds for the transformation of peace into war in class society.

Before it explodes, a bomb is a single entity in which opposites coexist in given conditions. The explosion takes place only when a new condition, ignition, is present. An analogous situation arises in all those natural phenomena which finally assume the form of open conflict to resolve old contradictions and produce new things.

61

It is highly important to grasp this fact. It enables us to understand that revolutions and revolutionary wars are inevitable in class society and that without them, it is impossible to accomplish any leap in social development and to overthrow the reactionary ruling classes and therefore impossible for the people to win political power. Communists must expose the deceitful propaganda of the reactionaries, such as the assertion that social revolution is unnecessary and impossible. They must firmly uphold the Marxist-Leninist theory of social revolution and enable the people to understand that social revolution is not only entirely necessary but also entirely practicable, and that the whole history of mankind and the triumph of the Soviet Union have confirmed this scientific truth.

However, we must make a concrete study of the circumstances of each specific struggle of opposites and should not arbitrarily apply the formula discussed above to everything. Contradiction and struggle are universal and absolute, but the methods of resolving contradictions, that is, the forms of struggle, differ according to the differences in the nature of the contradictions. Some contradictions are characterized by open antagonism, others are not. In accordance with the concrete development of things, some contradictions which were originally non-antagonistic develop into antagonistic ones, while others which were originally antagonistic develop into non-antagonistic ones.

As already mentioned, so long as classes exist, contradictions between correct and incorrect ideas in the Communist Party are reflections within the Party of class contradictions. At first, with regard to certain issues, such contradictions may not manifest themselves as antagonistic. But with the development of the class struggle, they may grow and become antagonistic. The history of the Communist Party of the Soviet Union shows us that the contradictions between the correct thinking of Lenin and Stalin and the fallacious thinking of Trotsky, Bukharin and others did not at first manifest themselves in an antagonistic form, but that later they did develop into antagonism. There are similar cases in the history of the Chinese Communist Party. At first the contradictions between the correct thinking of many of our Party comrades and the fallacious thinking of Chen Tu-hsiu, Chang Kuo-tao and others also did not manifest themselves in an antagonistic form, but later they did develop into antagonism. At present the contradiction between correct and incorrect thinking in our Party does not manifest itself in an antagonistic form, and if comrades who have committed mistakes can correct them, it will not develop into antagonism. Therefore, the Party must on the one hand wage a serious struggle against erroneous thinking, and on the other give the comrades who have committed errors ample opportunity to wake up. This being the case, excessive struggle is obviously inappropriate. But if the people who have committed errors persist in them and aggravate them, there is the possibility that this contradiction will develop into antagonism.

Economically, the contradiction between town and country is an extremely antagonistic one both in capitalist society, where under the rule of the bourgeoisie the towns ruthlessly plunder the countryside, and in the Kuomintang areas in China, where under the rule of foreign imperialism and the Chinese big comprador bourgeoisie the towns most rapaciously plunder the countryside. But in a socialist country and in our revolutionary base areas, this antagonistic contradiction has changed into one that is non-antagonistic; and when communist society is reached it will be abolished.

Lenin said, "Antagonism and contradiction are not at all one and the same. Under socialism, the first will disappear, the second will remain."[25] That is to say, antagonism is one form, but not the only form, of the struggle of opposites; the formula of antagonism cannot be arbitrarily applied everywhere.

VII. CONCLUSION

We may now say a few words to sum up. The law of contradiction in things, that is, the law of the unity of opposites, is the fundamental law of nature and of society and therefore also the fundamental law of thought. It stands opposed to the metaphysical world outlook. It represents a great revolution in the history of human knowledge. According to dialectical materialism, contradiction is present in all processes of objectively existing things and of subjective thought and permeates all these processes from beginning to end; this is the universality and absoluteness of contradiction. Each contradiction and each of its aspects have their respective characteristics; this is the particularity and relativity of contradiction. In given conditions, opposites possess identity, and consequently can coexist in a single entity and can transform themselves into each other; this again is the particularity and relativity of contradiction. But the struggle of opposites is ceaseless, it goes on both when the opposites are coexisting and when they are transforming themselves into each other, and becomes especially conspicuous when they are transforming themselves into one another; this again is the universality and absoluteness of contradiction. In studying the particularity and relativity of contradiction, we must give attention to the distinction between the principal contradiction and the non-principal contradictions and to the distinction between the principal aspect and the non-principal aspect of a contradiction; in studying the universality of contradiction and the struggle of opposites in contradiction, we must give attention to the distinction between the different forms of struggle. Otherwise we shall make mistakes. If, through study, we achieve a real understanding of the essentials explained above, we shall be able to demolish dogmatist ideas which are contrary to the basic principles of Marxism-Leninism and detrimental to our revolutionary cause, and our comrades with practical experience will be able to organize their experience into principles and avoid repeating empiricist errors. These are a few simple conclusions from our study of the law of contradiction.

NOTES

[1] V. I. Lenin, "Conspectus of Hegel's *Lectures on the History of Philosophy*", *Collected Works*, Russ. ed., Moscow, 1958, Vol. XXXVIII, p. 249.

[2] In his essay "On the Question of Dialectics", Lenin said, "The splitting in two of a single whole and the cognition of its contradictory parts (see the quotation from Philo on Heraclitus at the beginning of Section 3 'On Cognition' in Lassalle's book on Heraclitus) is the *essence* (one of the 'essentials', one of the principal, if not the principal, characteristics or features) of dialectics." (*Collected Works*, Russ. ed., Moscow, 1958, Vol. XXXVIII, p. 357.) In his "Conspectus of Hegel's *The Science of Logic*", he said, "In brief, dialectics can be defined as the doctrine of the unity of opposites. This grasps the kernel of dialectics, but it requires explanations and development." (*Ibid.*, p. 215.)

[3] V. I. Lenin, "On the Question of Dialectics", *Collected Works*, Russ. ed., Moscow, 1958, Vol. XXXVIII, p. 358.

[4] A saying of Tung Chung-shu (179-104 B.C.), a well-known exponent of Confucianism in the Han Dynasty.

[5] Frederick Engels, "Dialectics. Quantity and Quality", *Anti-Dühring*, Eng. ed., FLPH, Moscow, 1959, p. 166.

[6] V. I. Lenin, "On the Question of Dialectics", *Collected Works*, Russ. ed., Moscow, 1958, Vol. XXXVIII, pp. 357-58.

[7] Frederick Engels, *op. cit.*, pp. 166-67.

[8] V. I. Lenin, "On the Question of Dialectics", *Collected Works*, Russ. ed., Moscow, 1958, Vol. XXXVIII, p. 357.

[9] *Ibid.*, pp. 358-59.

[10] See "Problems of Strategy in China's Revolutionary War", Note 10, p. 251 of this volume.

[11] See *ibid.*, Note 2, p. 249 of this volume.

[12] Wei Cheng (A.D. 580-643) was a statesman and historian of the Tang Dynasty.

[13] *Shui Hu Chuan (Heroes of the Marshes)*, a famous 14th century Chinese novel, describes a peasant war towards the end of the Northern Sung Dynasty. Chu Village was in the vicinity of Liangshanpo, where Sung Chiang, leader of the peasant uprising and hero of the novel, established his base. Chu Chao-feng, the head of this village, was a despotic landlord.

[14] V. I. Lenin, "Once Again on the Trade Unions, the Present Situation and the Mistakes of Trotsky and Bukharin", *Selected Works*, Eng. ed., International Publishers, New York, 1943, Vol. IX, p. 66.

[15] V. I. Lenin, "What Is to Be Done?", *Collected Works*, Eng. ed., FLPH, Moscow, 1961, Vol. V, p. 369.

[16] V. I. Lenin, "Conspectus of Hegel's *The Science of Logic*", *Collected Works*, Russ. ed., Moscow, 1958, Vol. XXXVIII, pp. 97-98.

[17] *Shan Hai Ching (Book of Mountains and Seas)* was written in the era of the Warring States (403-221 B.C.). In one of its fables Kua Fu, a superman, pursued and overtook the sun. But he died of thirst, whereupon his staff was transformed into the forest of Teng.

[18] Yi is one of the legendary heroes of ancient China, famous for his archery. According to a legend in *Huai Nan Tzu*, compiled in the 2nd century B.C., there were ten suns in the sky in the days of Emperor Yao. To put an end to the damage to vegetation caused by these scorching suns, Emperor Yao ordered Yi to shoot them down. In another legend recorded by Wang Yi (2nd century A.D.), the archer is said to have shot down nine of the ten suns.

[19] *Hsi Yu Chi (Pilgrimage to the West)* is a 16th century novel, the hero of which is the monkey god Sun Wu-kung. He could miraculously change at will into seventy-two different shapes, such as a bird, a tree and a stone.

[20] The *Strange Tales of Liao Chai*, written by Pu Sung-ling in the 17th century, is a well-known collection of 431 tales, mostly about ghosts and fox spirits.

[21] Karl Marx, "Introduction to the Critique of Political Economy", *A Contribution to the Critique of Political Economy*, Eng. ed., Chicago, 1904, pp. 310-11.

[22] V. I. Lenin, "On the Question of Dialectics", *Collected Works*, Russ. ed., Moscow, 1958, Vol. XXXVIII, p. 358.

[23] The saying "Things that oppose each other also complement each other" first appeared in the *History of the Earlier Han Dynasty* by Pan Ku, a celebrated historian in the 1st century A.D. It has long been a popular saying.

[24] V. I. Lenin, "On the Question of Dialectics", *Collected Works*, Russ. ed., Moscow, 1958, Vol. XXXVIII, p. 358.

[25] V. I. Lenin, "Remarks on N. I. Bukharin's *Economics of the Transitional Period*", *Selected Works*, Russ. ed., Moscow-Leningrad, 1931, Vol. XI, p. 357.

ON NEW DEMOCRACY

ON NEW DEMOCRACY

January 1940

I. WHITHER CHINA?

A lively atmosphere has prevailed throughout the country ever since the War of Resistance began, there is a general feeling that a way out of the impasse has been found, and people no longer knit their brows in despair. Of late, however, the dust and din of compromise and anti-communism have once again filled the air, and once again the people are thrown into bewilderment. Most susceptible, and the first to be affected, are the intellectuals and the young students. The question once again arises: What is to be done? Whither China? On the occasion of the publication of *Chinese Culture*,[1] it may therefore be profitable to clarify the political and cultural trends in the country. I am a layman in matters of culture; I would like to study them, but have only just begun to do so. Fortunately, there are many comrades in Yenan who have written at length in this field, so that my rough and ready words may serve the same purpose as the beating of the gongs before a theatrical performance. Our observations may contain a grain of truth for the nation's advanced cultural workers and may serve as a modest spur to induce them to come forward with valuable contributions of their own, and we hope that they will join in the discussion to reach correct conclusions which will meet our national needs. To "seek truth from facts" is the scientific approach, and presumptuously to claim infallibility and lecture people will never settle anything. The troubles that have befallen our nation are extremely serious, and only a scientific approach and a spirit of responsibility can lead it on to the road of liberation. There is but one truth, and the question of whether or not one has arrived at it depends not on subjective boasting but on objective practice. The only yardstick of truth is the revolutionary practice of millions of people. This, I think, can be regarded as the attitude of *Chinese Culture.*

II. WE WANT TO BUILD A NEW CHINA

For many years we Communists have struggled for a cultural revolution as well as for a political and economic revolution, and our aim is to build a new society and a new state for the Chinese nation. That new society and new state will have not only a new politics and a new economy but a new culture. In other words, not only do we want to change a China that is politically oppressed and economically exploited into a China that is politically free and economically prosperous, we also want to change the China which is being kept ignorant and backward under the sway of the old culture into an enlightened and progressive China under the sway of a new culture. In short, we want to build a new China. Our aim in the cultural sphere is to build a new Chinese national culture.

III. CHINA'S HISTORICAL CHARACTERISTICS

We want to build a new national culture, but what kind of culture should it be?

Any given culture (as an ideological form) is a reflection of the politics and economics of a given society, and the former in turn has a tremendous influence and effect upon the latter; economics is the base and politics the concentrated expression of economics.[2] This is our fundamental view of the relation of culture to politics and economics and of the relation of politics to economics. It follows that the form of culture is first determined by the political and economic form, and only then does it operate on and influence the given political and economic form. Marx says, "It is not the consciousness of men that determines their being, but, on the contrary, their social being that determines their consciousness."[3] He also says, "The philosophers have only *interpreted* the world, in various ways; the point, however, is to *change* it."[4] For the first time in human history, these scientific formulations correctly solved the problem of the relationship between consciousness and existence, and they are the basic concepts underlying the dynamic revolutionary theory of knowledge as the reflection of reality which was later elaborated so profoundly by Lenin. These basic concepts must be kept in mind in our discussion of China's cultural problems.

Thus it is quite clear that the reactionary elements of the old national culture we want to eliminate are inseparable from the old national politics and economics, while the new national culture which we want to build up is inseparable from the new national politics and economics. The old politics and economics of the Chinese nation form the basis of its old culture, just as its new politics and economics will form the basis of its new culture.

What are China's old politics and economics? And what is her old culture?

From the Chou and Chin Dynasties onwards, Chinese society was feudal, as were its politics and its economy. And the dominant culture, reflecting the politics and economy, was feudal culture.

Since the invasion of foreign capitalism and the gradual growth of capitalist elements in Chinese society, the country has changed by degrees into a colonial, semi-colonial and semi-feudal society. China today is colonial in the Japanese-occupied areas and basically semi-colonial in the Kuomintang areas, and it is predominantly feudal or semi-feudal in both. Such, then, is the character of present-day Chinese society and the state of affairs in our country. The politics and the economy of this society are predominantly colonial, semi-colonial and semi-feudal, and the predominant culture, reflecting the politics and economy, is also colonial, semi-colonial and semi-feudal.

It is precisely against these predominant political, economic and cultural forms that our revolution is directed. What we want to get rid of is the old colonial, semi-colonial and semi-feudal politics and economy and the old culture in their service. And what we want to build up is their direct opposite, i.e., the new politics, the new economy and the new culture of the Chinese nation.

What, then, are the new politics and the new economy of the Chinese nation, and what is its new culture?

In the course of its history the Chinese revolution must go through two stages, first, the democratic revolution, and second, the socialist revolution, and by their very nature they are two different revolutionary processes. Here democracy does not belong to the old category — it is not the old democracy, but belongs to the new category — it is New Democracy.

It can thus be affirmed that China's new politics are the politics of New Democracy, that China's new economy is the economy of New Democracy and that China's new culture is the culture of New Democracy.

Such are the historical characteristics of the Chinese revolution at the present time. Any political party, group or person taking part in the Chinese revolution that fails to understand this will not be able to direct the revolution and lead it to victory, but will be cast aside by the people and left to grieve out in the cold.

IV. THE CHINESE REVOLUTION IS PART OF THE WORLD REVOLUTION

The historical characteristic of the Chinese revolution lies in its division into the two stages, democracy and socialism, the first being no longer democracy in general, but democracy of the Chinese type, a new and special type, namely, New Democracy. How, then, has this historical characteristic come into being? Has it been in existence for the past hundred years, or is it of recent origin?

A brief study of the historical development of China and of the world shows that this characteristic did not emerge immediately after the Opium War, but took shape later, after the first imperialist world war and the October Revolution in Russia. Let us now examine the process of its formation.

Clearly, it follows from the colonial, semi-colonial and semi-feudal character of present-day Chinese society that the Chinese revolution must be divided into two stages. The first step is to change the colonial, semi-colonial and semi-feudal form of society into an independent, democratic society. The second is to carry the revolution forward and build a socialist society. At present the Chinese revolution is taking the first step.

The preparatory period for the first step began with the Opium War in 1840, *i.e.*, when China's feudal society started changing into a semi-colonial and semi-feudal one. Then came the Movement of the Taiping Heavenly Kingdom, the Sino-French War, the Sino-Japanese

War, the Reform Movement of 1898, the Revolution of 1911, the May 4th Movement, the Northern Expedition, the War of the Agrarian Revolution and the present War of Resistance Against Japan. Together these have taken up a whole century and in a sense they represent that first step, being struggles waged by the Chinese people, on different occasions and in varying degrees, against imperialism and the feudal forces in order to build up an independent, democratic society and complete the first revolution. The Revolution of 1911 was in a fuller sense the beginning of that revolution. In its social character, this revolution is a bourgeois-democratic and not a proletarian-socialist revolution. It is still unfinished and still demands great efforts, because to this day its enemies are still very strong. When Dr. Sun Yat-sen said, "The revolution is not yet completed, all my comrades must struggle on", he was referring to the bourgeois-democratic revolution.

A change, however, occurred in China's bourgeois-democratic revolution after the outbreak of the first imperialist world war in 1914 and the founding of a socialist state on one-sixth of the globe as a result of the Russian October Revolution of 1917.

Before these events, the Chinese bourgeois-democratic revolution came within the old category of the bourgeois-democratic world revolution, of which it was a part.

Since these events, the Chinese bourgeois-democratic revolution has changed, it has come within the new category of bourgeois-democratic revolutions and, as far as the alignment of revolutionary forces is concerned, forms part of the proletarian-socialist world revolution.

Why? Because the first imperialist world war and the first victorious socialist revolution, the October Revolution, have changed the whole course of world history and ushered in a new era.

It is an era in which the world capitalist front has collapsed in one part of the globe (one-sixth of the world) and has fully revealed its decadence everywhere else, in which the remaining capitalist parts cannot survive without relying more than ever on the colonies and semi-colonies, in which a socialist state has been established and has proclaimed its readiness to give active support to the liberation movement of all colonies and semi-colonies, and in which the proletariat of the capitalist countries is steadily freeing itself from the social-imperialist influence of the social-democratic parties and has proclaimed its support for the liberation movement in the colonies and semi-colonies. In this era, any revolution in a colony or semi-colony that is directed against imperialism, *i.e.*, against the international bourgeoisie or international capitalism, no longer comes within the old category of the bourgeois-democratic world revolution, but within the new category. It is no longer part of the old bourgeois, or capitalist, world revolution, but is part of the new world revolution, the proletarian-socialist world revolution. Such revolutionary colonies and semi-colonies can no longer be regarded as allies of the counter-revolutionary front of world capitalism; they have become allies of the revolutionary front of world socialism.

Although such a revolution in a colonial and semi-colonial country is still fundamentally bourgeois-democratic in its social character during its first stage or first step, and although its objective mission is to clear the path for the development of capitalism, it is no longer a revolution of the old type led by the bourgeoisie with the aim of establishing a capitalist society and a state under bourgeois dictatorship. It belongs to the new type of revolution led by the proletariat with the aim, in the first stage, of establishing a new-democratic society and a state under the joint dictatorship of all the revolutionary classes. Thus this revolution actually serves the purpose of clearing a still wider path for the development of socialism. In the course of its progress, there may be a number of further sub-stages, because of changes on the enemy's side and within the ranks of our allies, but the fundamental character of the revolution remains unchanged.

Such a revolution attacks imperialism at its very roots, and is therefore not tolerated but opposed by imperialism. However, it is favoured by socialism and supported by the land of socialism and the socialist international proletariat.

Therefore, such a revolution inevitably becomes part of the proletarian-socialist world revolution.

The correct thesis that "the Chinese revolution is part of the world revolution" was put forward as early as 1924-27 during the period of China's First Great Revolution. It was put forward by the Chinese Communists and endorsed by all those taking part in the anti-imperialist and anti-feudal struggle of the time. However, the significance of this thesis was not fully expounded in those days, and consequently it was only vaguely understood.

The "world revolution" no longer refers to the old world revolution, for the old bourgeois world revolution has long been a thing of the past; it refers to the new world revolution, the socialist world revolution. Similarly, to form "part of" means to form part not

74

of the old bourgeois but of the new socialist revolution. This is a tremendous change unparalleled in the history of China and of the world.

This correct thesis advanced by the Chinese Communists is based on Stalin's theory.

As early as 1918, in an article commemorating the first anniversary of the October Revolution, Stalin wrote:

> The great world-wide significance of the October Revolution chiefly consists in the fact that:
>
> 1) It has widened the scope of the national question and converted it from the particular question of combating national oppression in Europe into the general question of emancipating the oppressed peoples, colonies and semi-colonies from imperialism;
>
> 2) It has opened up wide possibilities for their emancipation and the right paths towards it, has thereby greatly facilitated the cause of the emancipation of the oppressed peoples of the West and the East, and has drawn them into the common current of the victorious struggle against imperialism;
>
> 3) *It has thereby erected a bridge between the socialist West and the enslaved East,* having created a new front of revolutions *against* world imperialism, extending from the proletarians of the West, through the Russian Revolution, to the oppressed peoples of the East.[5]

Since writing this article, Stalin has again and again expounded the theory that revolutions in the colonies and semi-colonies have broken away from the old category and become part of the proletarian-socialist revolution. The clearest and most precise explanation is given in an article published on June 30, 1925, in which Stalin carried on a controversy with the Yugoslav nationalists of the time. Entitled "The National Question Once Again", it is included in a book translated by Chang Chung-shih and published under the title *Stalin on the National Question*. It contains the following passage:

> Semich refers to a passage in Stalin's pamphlet *Marxism and the National Question*, written at the end of 1912. There it says that "the national struggle under the conditions of *rising* capitalism is a struggle of the bourgeois classes among themselves". Evidently, by this Semich is trying to suggest that his formula defining the social significance of the national movement under the present

historical conditions is correct. But Stalin's pamphlet was written before the imperialist war, when the national question was not yet regarded by Marxists as a question of world significance, when the Marxists' fundamental demand for the right to self-determination was regarded not as part of the proletarian revolution, but as part of the bourgeois-democratic revolution. It would be ridiculous not to see that since then the international situation has radically changed, that the war, on the one hand, and the October Revolution in Russia, on the other, transformed the national question from a part of the bourgeois-democratic revolution into a part of the proletarian-socialist revolution. As far back as October 1916, in his article, "The Discussion on Self-Determination Summed Up", Lenin said that the main point of the national question, the right to self-determination, had ceased to be a part of the general democratic movement, that it had already become a component part of the general proletarian, socialist revolution. I do not even mention subsequent works on the national question by Lenin and by other representatives of Russian communism. After all this, what significance can Semich's reference to the passage in Stalin's pamphlet, written in the period of the *bourgeois*-democratic revolution in Russia, have at the present time, when, as a consequence of the new historical situation, we have entered a new epoch, the epoch of *proletarian* revolution? It can only signify that Semich quotes outside of space and time, without reference to the living historical situation, and thereby violates the most elementary requirements of dialectics, and ignores the fact that what is right for one historical situation may prove to be wrong in another historical situation.[6]

From this it can be seen that there are two kinds of world revolution, the first belonging to the bourgeois or capitalist category. The era of this kind of world revolution is long past, having come to an end as far back as 1914 when the first imperialist world war broke out, and more particularly in 1917 when the October Revolution took place. The second kind, namely, the proletarian-socialist world revolution, thereupon began. This revolution has the proletariat of the capitalist countries as its main force and the oppressed peoples of the colonies and semi-colonies as its allies. No matter what classes, parties or individuals in an oppressed nation join the revolution, and no matter whether they themselves are conscious of the point or understand it, so long as they oppose imperialism, their revolution becomes part of the proletarian-socialist world revolution and they become its allies.

Today, the Chinese revolution has taken on still greater significance. This is a time when the economic and political crises of capitalism are dragging the world more and more deeply into the Second World War, when the Soviet Union has reached the period of transition from socialism to communism and is capable of leading and helping the proletariat and oppressed nations of the whole world in their fight against imperialist war and capitalist reaction, when the proletariat of the capitalist countries is preparing to overthrow capitalism and establish socialism, and when the proletariat, the peasantry, the intelligentsia and other sections of the petty bourgeoisie in China have become a mighty independent political force under the leadership of the Chinese Communist Party. Situated as we are in this day and age, should we not make the appraisal that the Chinese revolution has taken on still greater world significance? I think we should. The Chinese revolution has become a very important part of the world revolution.

Although the Chinese revolution in this first stage (with its many sub-stages) is a new type of bourgeois-democratic revolution and is not yet itself a proletarian-socialist revolution in its social character, it has long become a part of the proletarian-socialist world revolution and is now even a very important part and a great ally of this world revolution. The first step or stage in our revolution is definitely not, and cannot be, the establishment of a capitalist society under the dictatorship of the Chinese bourgeoisie, but will result in the establishment of a new-democratic society under the joint dictatorship of all the revolutionary classes of China headed by the Chinese proletariat. The revolution will then be carried forward to the second stage, in which a socialist society will be established in China.

This is the fundamental characteristic of the Chinese revolution of today, of the new revolutionary process of the past twenty years (counting from the May 4th Movement of 1919), and its concrete living essence.

V.   THE POLITICS OF NEW DEMOCRACY

The new historical characteristic of the Chinese revolution is its division into two stages, the first being the new-democratic revolution.

How does this manifest itself concretely in internal political and economic relations? Let us consider the question.

Before the May 4th Movement of 1919 (which occurred after the first imperialist world war of 1914 and the Russian October Revolution of 1917), the petty bourgeoisie and the bourgeoisie (through their intellectuals) were the political leaders of the bourgeois-democratic revolution. The Chinese proletariat had not yet appeared on the political scene as an awakened and independent class force, but participated in the revolution only as a follower of the petty bourgeoisie and the bourgeoisie. Such was the case with the proletariat at the time of the Revolution of 1911.

After the May 4th Movement, the political leader of China's bourgeois-democratic revolution was no longer the bourgeoisie but the proletariat, although the national bourgeoisie continued to take part in the revolution. The Chinese proletariat rapidly became an awakened and independent political force as a result of its maturing and of the influence of the Russian Revolution. It was the Chinese Communist Party that put forward the slogan "Down with imperialism" and the thoroughgoing programme for the whole bourgeois-democratic revolution, and it was the Chinese Communist Party alone that carried out the Agrarian Revolution.

Being a bourgeoisie in a colonial and semi-colonial country and oppressed by imperialism, the Chinese national bourgeoisie retains a certain revolutionary quality at certain periods and to a certain degree — even in the era of imperialism — in its opposition to the foreign imperialists and the domestic governments of bureaucrats and warlords (instances of opposition to the latter can be found in the periods of the Revolution of 1911 and the Northern Expedition), and it may ally itself with the proletariat and the petty bourgeoisie against such enemies as it is ready to oppose. In this respect the Chinese bourgeoisie differs from the bourgeoisie of old tsarist Russia. Since tsarist Russia was a military-feudal imperialism which carried on aggression against other countries, the Russian bourgeoisie was entirely lacking in revolutionary quality. There, the task of the proletariat was to oppose the bourgeoisie, not to unite with it. But China's national bourgeoisie has a revolutionary quality at certain periods and to a certain degree, because China is a colonial and semi-colonial country which is a victim of aggression. Here, the task of the proletariat is to form a united front with the national bourgeoisie against imperialism and

78

the bureaucrat and warlord governments without overlooking its revolutionary quality.

At the same time, however, being a bourgeois class in a colonial and semi-colonial country and so being extremely flabby economically and politically, the Chinese national bourgeoisie also has another quality, namely, a proneness to conciliation with the enemies of the revolution. Even when it takes part in the revolution, it is unwilling to break with imperialism completely and, moreover, it is closely associated with the exploitation of the rural areas through land rent; thus it is neither willing nor able to overthrow imperialism, and much less the feudal forces, in a thorough way. So neither of the two basic problems or tasks of China's bourgeois-democratic revolution can be solved or accomplished by the national bourgeoisie. As for China's big bourgeoisie, which is represented by the Kuomintang, all through the long period from 1927 to 1937 it nestled in the arms of the imperialists and formed an alliance with the feudal forces against the revolutionary people. In 1927 and for some time afterwards, the Chinese national bourgeoisie also followed the counter-revolution. During the present anti-Japanese war, the section of the big bourgeoisie represented by Wang Ching-wei has capitulated to the enemy, which constitutes a fresh betrayal on the part of the big bourgeoisie. In this respect, then, the bourgeoisie in China differs from the earlier bourgeoisie of the European and American countries, and especially of France. When the bourgeoisie in those countries, and especially in France, was still in its revolutionary era, the bourgeois revolution was comparatively thorough, whereas the bourgeoisie in China lacks even this degree of thoroughness.

Possible participation in the revolution on the one hand and proneness to conciliation with the enemies of the revolution on the other — such is the dual character of the Chinese bourgeoisie, it faces both ways. Even the bourgeoisie in European and American history had shared this dual character. When confronted by a formidable enemy, they united with the workers and peasants against him, but when the workers and peasants awakened, they turned round to unite with the enemy against the workers and peasants. This is a general rule applicable to the bourgeoisie everywhere in the world, but the trait is more pronounced in the Chinese bourgeoisie.

In China, it is perfectly clear that whoever can lead the people in overthrowing imperialism and the forces of feudalism can win the people's confidence, because these two, and especially imperialism, are the mortal enemies of the people. Today, whoever can lead the people in driving out Japanese imperialism and introducing democratic government will be the saviours of the people. History has proved that the Chinese bourgeoisie cannot fulfil this responsibility, which inevitably falls upon the shoulders of the proletariat.

Therefore, the proletariat, the peasantry, the intelligentsia and the other sections of the petty bourgeoisie undoubtedly constitute the basic forces determining China's fate. These classes, some already awakened and others in the process of awakening, will necessarily become the basic components of the state and governmental structure in the democratic republic of China, with the proletariat as the leading force. The Chinese democratic republic which we desire to establish now must be a democratic republic under the joint dictatorship of all anti-imperialist and anti-feudal people led by the proletariat, that is, a new-democratic republic, a republic of the genuinely revolutionary new Three People's Principles with their Three Great Policies.

This new-democratic republic will be different from the old European-American form of capitalist republic under bourgeois dictatorship, which is the old democratic form and already out of date. On the other hand, it will also be different from the socialist republic of the Soviet type under the dictatorship of the proletariat which is already flourishing in the U.S.S.R., and which, moreover, will be established in all the capitalist countries and will undoubtedly become the dominant form of state and governmental structure in all the industrially advanced countries. However, for a certain historical period, this form is not suitable for the revolutions in the colonial and semi-colonial countries. During this period, therefore, a third form of state must be adopted in the revolutions of all colonial and semi-colonial countries, namely, the new-democratic republic. This form suits a certain historical period and is therefore transitional; nevertheless, it is a form which is necessary and cannot be dispensed with.

Thus the numerous types of state system in the world can be reduced to three basic kinds according to the class character of their political power: (1) republics under bourgeois dictatorship; (2) republics under the dictatorship of the proletariat; and (3) republics under the joint dictatorship of several revolutionary classes.

The first kind comprises the old democratic states. Today, after the outbreak of the second imperialist war, there is hardly a trace of democracy in many of the capitalist countries, which have come or are coming under the bloody militarist dictatorship of the bourgeoisie.

Certain countries under the joint dictatorship of the landlords and the bourgeoisie can be grouped with this kind.

The second kind exists in the Soviet Union, and the conditions for its birth are ripening in capitalist countries. In the future, it will be the dominant form throughout the world for a certain period.

The third kind is the transitional form of state to be adopted in the revolutions of the colonial and semi-colonial countries. Each of these revolutions will necessarily have specific characteristics of its own, but these will be minor variations on a general theme. So long as they are revolutions in colonial or semi-colonial countries, their state and governmental structure will of necessity be basically the same, *i.e.*, a new-democratic state under the joint dictatorship of several anti-imperialist classes. In present-day China, the anti-Japanese united front represents the new-democratic form of state. It is anti-Japanese and anti-imperialist; it is also a united front, an alliance of several revolutionary classes. But unfortunately, despite the fact that the war has been going on for so long, the work of introducing democracy has hardly started in most of the country outside the democratic anti-Japanese base areas under the leadership of the Communist Party, and the Japanese imperialists have exploited this fundamental weakness to stride into our country. If nothing is done about it, our national future will be gravely imperilled.

The question under discussion here is that of the "state system". After several decades of wrangling since the last years of the Ching Dynasty, it has still not been cleared up. Actually it is simply a question of the status of the various social classes within the state. The bourgeoisie, as a rule, conceals the problem of class status and carries out its one-class dictatorship under the "national" label. Such concealment is of no advantage to the revolutionary people and the matter should be clearly explained to them. The term "national" is all right, but it must not include counter-revolutionaries and traitors. The kind of state we need today is a dictatorship of all the revolutionary classes over the counter-revolutionaries and traitors.

> The so-called democratic system in modern states is usually monopolized by the bourgeoisie and has become simply an instrument for oppressing the common people. On the other hand, the Kuomintang's Principle of Democracy means a democratic system shared by all the common people and not privately owned by the few.

Such was the solemn declaration made in the Manifesto of the First National Congress of the Kuomintang, held in 1924 during the period of Kuomintang-Communist co-operation. For sixteen years the Kuomintang has violated this declaration and as a result it has created the present grave national crisis. This is a gross blunder, which we hope the Kuomintang will correct in the cleansing flames of the anti-Japanese war.

As for the question of "the system of government", this is a matter of how political power is organized, the form in which one social class or another chooses to arrange its apparatus of political power to oppose its enemies and protect itself. There is no state which does not have an appropriate apparatus of political power to represent it. China may now adopt a system of people's congresses, from the national people's congress down to the provincial, county, district and township people's congresses, with all levels electing their respective governmental bodies. But if there is to be a proper representation for each revolutionary class according to its status in the state, a proper expression of the people's will, a proper direction for revolutionary struggles and a proper manifestation of the spirit of New Democracy, then a system of really universal and equal suffrage, irrespective of sex, creed, property or education, must be introduced. Such is the system of democratic centralism. Only a government based on democratic centralism can fully express the will of all the revolutionary people and fight the enemies of the revolution most effectively. There must be a spirit of refusal to be "privately owned by the few" in the government and the army; without a genuinely democratic system this cannot be attained and the system of government and the state system will be out of harmony.

The state system, a joint dictatorship of all the revolutionary classes and the system of government, democratic centralism — these constitute the politics of New Democracy, the republic of New Democracy, the republic of the anti-Japanese united front, the republic of the new Three People's Principles with their Three Great Policies, the Republic of China in reality as well as in name. Today we have a Republic of China in name but not in reality, and our present task is to create the reality that will fit the name.

Such are the internal political relations which a revolutionary China, a China fighting Japanese aggression, should and must establish without fail; such is the orientation, the only correct orientation, for our present work of national reconstruction.

VI. THE ECONOMY OF NEW DEMOCRACY

If such a republic is to be established in China, it must be new-democratic not only in its politics but also in its economy.

It will own the big banks and the big industrial and commercial enterprises.

> Enterprises, such as banks, railways and airlines, whether Chinese-owned or foreign-owned, which are either monopolistic in character or too big for private management, shall be operated and administered by the state, so that private capital cannot dominate the livelihood of the people: this is the main principle of the regulation of capital.

This is another solemn declaration in the Manifesto of the Kuomintang's First National Congress held during the period of Kuomintang-Communist co-operation, and it is the correct policy for the economic structure of the new-democratic republic. In the new-democratic republic under the leadership of the proletariat, the state enterprises will be of a socialist character and will constitute the leading force in the whole national economy, but the republic will neither confiscate capitalist private property in general nor forbid the development of such capitalist production as does not "dominate the livelihood of the people", for China's economy is still very backward.

The republic will take certain necessary steps to confiscate the land of the landlords and distribute it to those peasants having little or no land, carry out Dr. Sun Yat-sen's slogan of "land to the tiller", abolish feudal relations in the rural areas, and turn the land over to the private ownership of the peasants. A rich peasant economy will be allowed in the rural areas. Such is the policy of "equalization of landownership". "Land to the tiller" is the correct slogan for this policy. In general, socialist agriculture will not be established at this stage, though various types of co-operative enterprises developed on the basis of "land to the tiller" will contain elements of socialism.

China's economy must develop along the path of the "regulation of capital" and the "equalization of landownership", and must never be "privately owned by the few"; we must never permit the few capitalists and landlords to "dominate the livelihood of the people"; we must never establish a capitalist society of the European-American type or allow the old semi-feudal society to survive. Whoever dares to go counter to this line of advance will certainly not succeed but will run into a brick wall.

Such are the internal economic relations which a revolutionary China, a China fighting Japanese aggression, must and necessarily will establish.

Such is the economy of New Democracy.

And the politics of New Democracy are the concentrated expression of the economy of New Democracy.

VII. REFUTATION OF BOURGEOIS DICTATORSHIP

More than 90 per cent of the people are in favour of a republic of this kind with its new-democratic politics and new-democratic economy; there is no alternative road.

What about the road to a capitalist society under bourgeois dictatorship? To be sure, that was the old road taken by the European and American bourgeoisie, but whether one likes it or not, neither the international nor the domestic situation allows China to do the same.

Judging by the international situation, that road is blocked. In its fundamentals, the present international situation is one of a struggle between capitalism and socialism, in which capitalism is on the downgrade and socialism on the upgrade. In the first place international capitalism, or imperialism, will not permit the establishment in China of a capitalist society under bourgeois dictatorship. Indeed the history of modern China is a history of imperialist aggression, of imperialist opposition to China's independence and to her development of capitalism. Earlier revolutions failed in China because imperialism strangled them, and innumerable revolutionary martyrs died, bitterly lamenting the non-fulfilment of their mission. Today a powerful Japanese imperialism is forcing its way into China and wants to reduce her to a colony; it is not China that is developing Chinese capitalism but Japan that is developing Japanese capitalism in our country; and it is not the Chinese bourgeoisie but the Japanese bourgeoisie that is exercising dictatorship in our country. True enough, this is the period of the final struggle of dying imperialism — imperialism is "moribund capitalism".[7] But just because it is dying, it is all the more dependent on colonies and semi-colonies for survival and will certainly not allow any colony or semi-colony to establish anything like a capitalist society

84

under the dictatorship of its own bourgeoisie. Just because Japanese imperialism is bogged down in serious economic and political crises, just because it is dying, it must invade China and reduce her to a colony, thereby blocking the road to bourgeois dictatorship and national capitalism in China.

In the second place, socialism will not permit it. All the imperialist powers in the world are our enemies, and China cannot possibly gain her independence without the assistance of the land of socialism and the international proletariat. That is, she cannot do so without the help of the Soviet Union and the help which the proletariat of Japan, Britain, the United States, France, Germany, Italy and other countries provide through their struggles against capitalism. Although no one can say that the victory of the Chinese revolution must wait upon the victory of the revolution in all of these countries, or in one or two of them, there is no doubt that we cannot win without the added strength of their proletariat. In particular, Soviet assistance is absolutely indispensable for China's final victory in the War of Resistance. Refuse Soviet assistance, and the revolution will fail. Don't the anti-Soviet campaigns from 1927 onwards[8] provide an extraordinarily clear lesson? The world today is in a new era of wars and revolutions, an era in which capitalism is unquestionably dying and socialism is unquestionably prospering. In these circumstances, would it not be sheer fantasy to desire the establishment in China of a capitalist society under bourgeois dictatorship after the defeat of imperialism and feudalism?

Even though the petty Kemalist dictatorship of the bourgeoisie[9] did emerge in Turkey after the first imperialist world war and the October Revolution owing to certain specific conditions (the bourgeoisie's success in repelling Greek aggression and the weakness of the proletariat), there can be no second Turkey, much less a "Turkey" with a population of 450 million, after World War II and the accomplishment of socialist construction in the Soviet Union. In the specific conditions of China (the flabbiness of the bourgeoisie with its proneness to conciliation and the strength of the proletariat with its revolutionary thoroughness), things just never work out so easily as in Turkey. Did not some members of the Chinese bourgeoisie clamour for Kemalism after the First Great Revolution failed in 1927? But where is China's Kemal? And where are China's bourgeois dictatorship and capitalist society? Besides, even Kemalist Turkey eventually had to throw herself into the arms of Anglo-French imperialism, becoming more and more of a semi-colony and part of the reactionary imperialist world. In the international situation of today, the "heroes" in the colonies and semi-colonies either line up on the imperialist front and become part of the forces of world counter-revolution, or they line up on the anti-imperialist front and become part of the forces of world revolution. They must do one or the other, for there is no third choice.

Judging by the domestic situation, too, the Chinese bourgeoisie should have learned its lesson by now. No sooner had the strength of the proletariat and of the peasant and other petty bourgeois masses brought the revolution of 1927 to victory than the capitalist class, headed by the big bourgeoisie, kicked the masses aside, seized the fruits of the revolution, formed a counter-revolutionary alliance with imperialism and the feudal forces, and strained themselves to the limit in a war of "Communist suppression" for ten years. But what was the upshot? Today, when a powerful enemy has penetrated deep into our territory and the anti-Japanese war has been going on for two years, is it possible that there are still people who want to copy the obsolete recipes of the European and American bourgeoisie? A decade was spent on "suppressing the Communists" out of existence, but no capitalist society under bourgeois dictatorship was "suppressed" into existence. Is it possible that there are still people who want to have another try? True, a "one-party dictatorship" was "suppressed" into existence through the decade of "Communist suppression", but it is a semi-colonial and semi-feudal dictatorship. What is more, at the end of four years of "Communist suppression" (from 1927 to the Incident of September 18, 1931), "Manchukuo" was "suppressed" into existence and in 1937, after another six years of such "suppression", the Japanese imperialists made their way into China south of the Great Wall. Today if anyone wants to carry on "suppression" for another decade, it would mean a new type of "Communist suppression", somewhat different from the old. But is there not one fleet-footed person who has already outstripped everyone else and boldly undertaken this new enterprise of "Communist suppression"? Yes, Wang Ching-wei, who has become the new-style anti-Communist celebrity. Anyone who wishes to join his gang can please himself; but wouldn't that turn out to be an added embarrassment when talking big about bourgeois dictatorship, capitalist society, Kemalism, a modern state, a one-party dictatorship, "one doctrine", and so on and so forth? And if, instead of joining the Wang Ching-wei gang, someone wants to come into the "fight Japan" camp of the people but imagines that

86

once the war is won he will be able to kick aside the people fighting Japan, seize the fruits of the victory of the fight against Japan and establish a "perpetual one-party dictatorship", isn't he just day-dreaming? "Fight Japan!" "Fight Japan!" But who is doing the fighting? Without the workers and the peasants and other sections of the petty bourgeoisie, you cannot move a step. Anyone who still dares to try and kick them aside will himself be crushed. Hasn't this, too, become a matter of common sense? But the die-hards among the Chinese bourgeoisie (I am referring solely to the die-hards) seem to have learned nothing in the past twenty years. Aren't they still shouting: "Restrict communism", "Corrode communism" and "Combat communism"? Haven't we seen "Measures for Restricting the Activities of Alien Parties" followed by "Measures for Dealing with the Alien Party Problem" and still later by "Directives for Dealing with the Alien Party Problem"? Heavens! With all this "restricting" and "dealing with" going on, one wonders what kind of future they are preparing for our nation and for themselves! We earnestly and sincerely advise these gentlemen: Open your eyes, take a good look at China and the world, see how things stand inside as well as outside the country, and do not repeat your mistakes. If you persist in your mistakes, the future of our nation will of course be disastrous, but I am sure things will not go well with you either. This is absolutely true, absolutely certain. Unless the die-hards among the Chinese bourgeoisie wake up, their future will be far from bright — they will only bring about their own destruction. Therefore we hope that China's anti-Japanese united front will be maintained and that, with the co-operation of all instead of the monopoly of a single clique, the anti-Japanese cause will be brought to victory; it is the only good policy — any other policy is bad. This is the sincere advice we Communists are giving, and do not blame us for not having forewarned you.

"If there is food, let everyone share it." This old Chinese saying contains much truth. Since we all share in fighting the enemy, we should all share in eating, we should all share in the work to be done, and we should all share access to education. Such attitudes as "I and I alone will take everything" and "no one dare harm me" are nothing but the old tricks of feudal lords which simply will not work in the Nineteen Forties.

We Communists will never push aside anyone who is revolutionary; we shall persevere in the united front and practise long-term co-operation with all those classes, strata, political parties and groups and individuals that are willing to fight Japan to the end. But it will not do if certain people want to push aside the Communist Party; it will not do if they want to split the united front. China must keep on fighting Japan, uniting and moving forward, and we cannot tolerate anyone who tries to capitulate, cause splits or move backward.

VIII. REFUTATION OF "LEFT" PHRASE-MONGERING

If the capitalist road of bourgeois dictatorship is out of the question, then is it possible to take the socialist road of proletarian dictatorship?

No, that is not possible either.

Without a doubt, the present revolution is the first step, which will develop into the second step, that of socialism, at a later date. And China will attain true happiness only when she enters the socialist era. But today is not yet the time to introduce socialism. The present task of the revolution in China is to fight imperialism and feudalism, and socialism is out of the question until this task is completed. The Chinese revolution cannot avoid taking the two steps, first of New Democracy and then of socialism. Moreover, the first step will need quite a long time and cannot be accomplished overnight. We are not utopians and cannot divorce ourselves from the actual conditions confronting us.

Certain malicious propagandists, deliberately confusing these two distinct revolutionary stages, advocate the so-called theory of a single revolution in order to prove that the Three People's Principles apply to all kinds of revolutions and that communism therefore loses its *raison d'être*. Utilizing this "theory", they frantically oppose communism and the Communist Party, the Eighth Route and New Fourth Armies, and the Shensi-Kansu-Ningsia Border Region. Their real purpose is to root out all revolution, to oppose a thoroughgoing bourgeois-democratic revolution and thoroughgoing resistance to Japan and to prepare public opinion for their capitulation to the Japanese aggressors. This is deliberately being fostered by the Japanese imperialists. Since their occupation of Wuhan, they have come to realize that military force alone cannot subjugate China and have therefore resorted to political offensives and economic blandishments. Their political offensives consist in tempting wavering elements in the anti-Japanese camp, splitting the united front and undermining Kuomintang-Communist co-operation. Their economic blandishments take the form of the so-called joint industrial enterprises. In central and southern China the Japanese aggressors are allowing Chinese capitalists to invest 51 per cent of the capital in such enterprises, with Japanese capital making up the other 49 per cent; in northern China they are allowing Chinese capitalists to invest 49 per cent of the capital, with Japanese capital making up the other 51 per cent. The Japanese invaders have also promised to restore the former assets of the Chinese capitalists to them in the form of capital shares in the investment. At the prospect of profits, some conscienceless capitalists forget all moral principles and itch to have a go. One section, represented by Wang Ching-wei, has already capitulated. Another section lurking in the anti-Japanese camp would also like to cross over. But, with the cowardice of thieves, they fear that the Communists will block their exit and, what is more, that the common people will brand them as traitors. So they have put their heads together and decided to prepare the ground in cultural circles and through the press. Having determined on their policy, they have lost no time in hiring some "metaphysics-mongers"[10] plus a few Trotskyites who, brandishing their pens like lances, are tilting in all directions and creating bedlam. Hence the whole bag of tricks for deceiving those who do not know what is going on in the world around them — the "theory of a single revolu-tion", the tales that communism does not suit the national conditions of China, that there is no need for a Communist Party in China, that the Eighth Route and the New Fourth Armies are sabotaging the anti-Japanese war and are merely moving about without fighting, that the Shensi-Kansu-Ningsia Border Region is a feudal separatist regime, that the Communist Party is disobedient, dissident, intriguing and disruptive — and all for the purpose of providing the capitalists with good grounds for getting their 49 or 51 per cent and selling out the nation's interests to the enemy at the opportune moment. This is "stealing the beams and pillars and replacing them with rotten timbers" — preparing the public mind for their projected capitulation. Thus, these gentlemen who, in all apparent seriousness, are pushing the "theory of a single revolution" to oppose communism and the Communist Party are out for nothing but their 49 or 51 per cent. How they must have cudgelled their brains! The "theory of a single revolution" is simply a theory of no revolution at all, and that is the heart of the matter.

But there are other people, apparently with no evil intentions, who are misled by the "theory of a single revolution" and the fanciful notion of "accomplishing both the political revolution and the social revolution at one stroke"; they do not understand that our revolution is divided into stages, that we can only proceed to the next stage of revolution after accomplishing the first, and that there is no such thing as "accomplishing both at one stroke". Their approach is likewise very harmful because it confuses the steps to be taken in the revolution and weakens the effort directed towards the current task. It is correct and in accord with the Marxist theory of revolutionary development to say of the two revolutionary stages that the first provides the conditions for the second and that the two must be consecutive, without allowing any intervening stage of bourgeois dictatorship. However, it is a utopian view rejected by true revolutionaries to say that the democratic revolution does not have a specific task and period of its own but can be merged and accomplished simultaneously with another task, *i.e.*, the socialist task (which can only be carried out in another period), and this is what they call "accomplishing both at one stroke".

IX. REFUTATION OF THE DIE-HARDS

The bourgeois die-hards in their turn come forward and say: "Well, you Communists have postponed the socialist system to a later stage and have declared, 'The Three People's Principles being what China needs today, our Party is ready to fight for their complete realization.'[11] All right then, fold up your communism for the time being." A fearful hullabaloo has recently been raised with this sort of argument in the form of the "one doctrine" theory. In essence it is the howl of the die-hards for bourgeois despotism. Out of courtesy, however, we may simply describe it as totally lacking in common sense.

Communism is at once a complete system of proletarian ideology and a new social system. It is different from any other ideology or social system, and is the most complete, progressive, revolutionary and rational system in human history. The ideological and social system of feudalism has a place only in the museum of history. The ideological and social system of capitalism has also become a museum piece in one part of the world (in the Soviet Union), while in other countries it resembles "a dying person who is sinking fast, like the sun setting beyond the western hills", and will soon be relegated to the museum. The communist ideological and social system alone is full of youth and vitality, sweeping the world with the momentum of an avalanche and the force of a thunderbolt. The introduction of scientific communism into China has opened new vistas for people and has changed the face of the Chinese revolution. Without communism to guide it, China's democratic revolution cannot possibly succeed, let alone move on to the next stage. This is the reason why the bourgeois die-hards are so loudly demanding that communism be "folded up". But it must not be "folded up", for once communism is "folded up", China will be doomed. The whole world today depends on communism for its salvation, and China is no exception.

Everybody knows that the Communist Party has an immediate and a future programme, a minimum and a maximum programme, with regard to the social system it advocates. For the present period, New Democracy, and for the future, socialism; these are two parts of an organic whole, guided by one and the same communist ideology. Is it not, therefore, in the highest degree absurd to clamour for communism to be "folded up" on the ground that the Communist Party's minimum programme is in basic agreement with the political tenets of the Three People's Principles? It is precisely because of this basic agreement between the two that we Communists find it possible to recognize "the Three People's Principles as the political basis for the anti-Japanese united front" and to acknowledge that "the Three People's Principles being what China needs today, our Party is ready to fight for their complete realization"; otherwise no such possibility would exist. Here we have a united front between communism and the Three People's Principles in the stage of the democratic revolution, the kind of united front Dr. Sun Yat-sen had in mind when he said: "Communism is the good friend of the Three People's Principles."[12] To reject communism is in fact to reject the united front. The die-hards have concocted absurd arguments for the rejection of communism just because they want to reject the united front and practise their one-party doctrine.

Moreover, the "one doctrine" theory is an absurdity. So long as classes exist, there will be as many doctrines as there are classes, and even various groups in the same class may have their different doctrines. Since the feudal class has a feudal doctrine, the bourgeoisie a capitalist doctrine, the Buddhists Buddhism, the Christians

91

Christianity and the peasants polytheism, and since in recent years, some people have also advocated Kemalism, fascism, vitalism,[13] the "doctrine of distribution according to labour",[14] and what not, why then cannot the proletariat have its communism? Since there are countless "isms", why should the cry of "Fold it up!" be raised at the sight of communism alone? Frankly, "folding it up" will not work. Let us rather have a contest. If communism is beaten, we Communists will admit defeat in good grace. But if not, then let all that stuff about "one doctrine", which violates the Principle of Democracy, be "folded up" as soon as possible.

To avoid misunderstanding and for the edification of the die-hards, it is necessary to show clearly where the Three People's Principles and communism do coincide and where they do not.

Comparison of the two reveals both similarities and differences.

First for the similarities. They are to be found in the basic political programme of both doctrines during the stage of the bourgeois-democratic revolution in China. The three political tenets of the revolutionary Three People's Principles of Nationalism, Democracy and the People's Livelihood as reinterpreted by Dr. Sun Yat-sen in 1924 are basically similar to the communist political programme for the stage of the democratic revolution in China. Because of these similarities and because of the carrying out of the Three People's Principles, the united front of the two doctrines and the two parties came into existence. It is wrong to ignore this aspect.

Next for the differences. (1) There is a difference in part of the programme for the stage of the democratic revolution. The communist programme for the whole course of the democratic revolution includes full rights for the people, the eight-hour working day and a thorough agrarian revolution, whereas the Three People's Principles do not. Unless these points are added to the Three People's Principles and there is the readiness to carry them out, the two democratic programmes are only basically the same and cannot be described as altogether the same. (2) Another difference is that one includes the stage of the socialist revolution, and the other does not. Communism envisages the stage of the socialist revolution beyond the stage of the democratic revolution, and hence, beyond its minimum programme it has a maximum programme, i.e., the programme for the attainment of socialism and communism. The Three People's Principles which envisage only the stage of the democratic revolution and not the stage of the socialist revolution have only a minimum programme and not a maximum programme, *i.e.*, they have no programme for the establishment of socialism and communism. (3) There is the difference in world outlook. The world outlook of communism is dialectical and historical materialism, while the Three People's Principles explain history in terms of the people's livelihood, which in essence is a dualist or idealist outlook; the two world outlooks are opposed to each other. (4) There is the difference in revolutionary thoroughness. With communists, theory and practice go together, *i.e.*, communists possess revolutionary thoroughness. With the followers of the Three People's Principles, except for those completely loyal to the revolution and to truth, theory and practice do not go together and their deeds contradict their words, *i.e.*, they lack revolutionary thoroughness. The above are the differences between the two. They distinguish communists from the followers of the Three People's Principles. It is undoubtedly very wrong to ignore this distinction and see only the aspect of unity and not of contradiction.

Once all this is understood, it is easy to see what the bourgeois die-hards have in mind when they demand that communism be "folded up". If it does not mean bourgeois despotism, then there is no sense to it at all.

X. THE THREE PEOPLE'S PRINCIPLES, OLD AND NEW

The bourgeois die-hards have no understanding whatsoever of historical change; their knowledge is so poor that it is practically non-existent. They do not know the difference either between communism and the Three People's Principles or between the new Three People's Principles and the old.

We Communists recognize "the Three People's Principles as the political basis for the Anti-Japanese National United Front", we acknowledge that "the Three People's Principles being what China needs today, our Party is ready to fight for their complete realization", and we admit the basic agreement between the communist minimum programme and the political tenets of the Three People's Principles. But which kind of Three People's Principles? The Three People's Principles as reinterpreted by Dr. Sun Yat-sen in the Manifesto of the First National Congress of the Kuomintang, and no other. I wish the die-hard gentlemen would spare a moment from the work of "restricting communism", "corroding communism" and "combating communism", in which they are so gleefully engaged, to glance through this manifesto. In the manifesto Dr. Sun Yat-sen said: "Here is the true interpretation of the Kuomintang's Three People's Principles." Hence these are the only genuine Three People's Principles and all others are spurious. The only "true interpretation" of the Three People's Principles is the one contained in the Manifesto of the First National Congress of the Kuomintang, and all other interpretations are false. Presumably this is no Communist fabrication, for many Kuomintang members and I myself personally witnessed the adoption of the manifesto.

The manifesto marks off the two epochs in the history of the Three People's Principles. Before it, they belonged to the old category; they were the Three People's Principles of the old bourgeois-democratic revolution in a semi-colony, the Three People's Principles of old democracy, the old Three People's Principles.

After it, they came within the new category; they became the Three People's Principles of the new bourgeois-democratic revolution in a semi-colony, the Three People's Principles of New Democracy, the new Three People's Principles. These and these alone are the revolutionary Three People's Principles of the new period.

The revolutionary Three People's Principles of the new period, the new or genuine Three People's Principles, embody the Three Great Policies of alliance with Russia, co-operation with the Communist Party and assistance to the peasants and workers. Without each and every one of these Three Great Policies, the Three People's Principles become either false or incomplete in the new period.

In the first place, the revolutionary, new or genuine Three People's Principles must include alliance with Russia. As things are today, it is perfectly clear that unless there is the policy of alliance with Russia, with the land of socialism, there will inevitably be a policy of alliance with imperialism, with the imperialist powers. Is this not exactly what happened after 1927? Once the conflict between the socialist Soviet Union and the imperialist powers grows sharper, China will have to take her stand on one side or the other. This is an inevitable trend. Is it possible to avoid leaning to either side? No, that is an illusion. The whole world will be swept into one or the other of these two fronts, and "neutrality" will then be merely a deceptive term. Especially is this true of China which, fighting an imperialist power that has penetrated deep into her territory, cannot conceive of ultimate victory without the assistance of the Soviet Union. If alliance with Russia is sacrificed for the sake of alliance with imperialism, the word "revolutionary" will have to be expunged from the Three People's Principles, which will then become reactionary. In the last analysis, there can be no "neutral" Three People's Principles; they can only be either revolutionary or counter-revolutionary. Would it not be more heroic to "fight against attacks from both sides"[15] as Wang Ching-wei once remarked, and to have the kind of Three People's Principles that serves this "fight"? Unfortunately, even its inventor Wang Ching-wei himself has abandoned (or "folded up") this kind of Three People's Principles, for he has adopted the Three People's Principles of alliance with imperialism. If it is argued that there is a difference between Eastern and Western imperialism, and that, unlike Wang Ching-wei who has allied himself with Eastern imperialism, one should ally oneself with some of the Western imperialists to march eastward and attack, then would not such conduct be quite revolutionary? However, whether you like it or not, the Western imperialists are determined to oppose the Soviet Union and communism, and if you ally yourself with them, they will ask you to march northward and attack, and your revolution will come to nothing. All these circumstances make it essential for the revolutionary, new and genuine Three People's Principles to include alliance with Russia, and under no circumstances alliance with imperialism against Russia.

In the second place, the revolutionary, new and genuine Three People's Principles must include co-operation with the Communist Party. Either you co-operate with the Communist Party or you oppose it. Opposition to communism is the policy of the Japanese imperialists and Wang Ching-wei, and if that is what you want, very well, they will invite you to join their Anti-Communist Company. But wouldn't that look suspiciously like turning traitor? You may say, "I am not following Japan, but some other country." That is just ridiculous. No matter whom you follow, the moment you oppose the Communist Party you become a traitor, because you can no longer resist Japan. If you say, "I am going to oppose the Communist Party independently", that is arrant nonsense. How can the "heroes" in a colony or semi-colony tackle a counter-revolutionary job of this magnitude without depending on the strength of imperialism? For ten long years, virtually all the imperialist forces in the world were enlisted against the Communist Party, but in vain. How can you suddenly oppose it "independently"?

Some people outside the Border Region, we are told, are now saying: "Opposing the Communist Party is good, but you can never succeed in it." This remark, if it is not simply hearsay, is only half wrong, for what "good" is there in opposing the Communist Party? But the other half is true, you certainly can "never succeed in it". Basically, the reason lies not with the Communists but with the common people, who like the Communist Party and do not like "opposing" it. If you oppose the Communist Party at a juncture when our national enemy is penetrating deep into our territory, the people will be after your hide; they will certainly show you no mercy. This much is certain, whoever wants to oppose the Communist Party must be prepared to be ground to dust. If you are not keen on being ground to dust, you had certainly better drop this opposition. This is our sincere advice to all the anti-Communist "heroes". Thus it is as clear as can be that the Three People's Principles of today must include co-operation with the Communist Party, or otherwise those Principles will perish. It is a question of life and death for the Three People's Principles. Co-operating with the Communist Party, they will survive; opposing the Communist Party, they will perish. Can anyone prove the contrary?

In the third place, the revolutionary, new and genuine Three People's Principles must include the policy of assisting the peasants and workers. Rejection of this policy, failure whole-heartedly to assist the peasants and workers or failure to carry out the behest in Dr. Sun Yat-sen's Testament to "arouse the masses of the people", amounts to preparing the way for the defeat of the revolution, and one's own defeat into the bargain. Stalin has said that *"in essence, the national question is a peasant question"*.[16] This means that the Chinese revolution is essentially a peasant revolution and that the resistance to Japan now going on is essentially peasant resistance. Essentially, the politics of New Democracy means giving the peasants their rights. The new and genuine Three People's Principles are essentially the principles of a peasant revolution. Essentially, mass culture means raising the cultural level of the peasants. The anti-Japanese war is essentially a peasant war. We are now living in a time when the "principle of going up into the hills"[17] applies; meetings, work, classes, newspaper publication, the writing of books, theatrical performances — everything is done up in the hills, and all essentially for the sake of the peasants. And essentially it is the peasants who provide everything that sustains the resistance to Japan and keeps us going. By "essentially" we mean basically, not ignoring the other sections of the people, as Stalin himself has explained. As every schoolboy knows, 80 per cent of China's population are peasants. So the peasant problem becomes the basic problem of the Chinese revolution and the strength of the peasants is the main strength of the Chinese revolution. In the Chinese population the workers rank second to the peasants in number. There are several million industrial workers in China and several tens of millions of handicraft workers and agricultural labourers. China cannot live without her workers in the various industries, because they are the producers in the industrial sector of the economy. And the revolution cannot succeed without the modern industrial working class, because it is the leader of the Chinese revolution and is the most revolutionary class. In these circumstances, the revolutionary, new and genuine Three People's Principles must include the policy of assisting the peasants and workers. Any other kind of Three People's Principles which lack this policy, do not give the peasants and workers whole-hearted assistance or do not carry out the behest to "arouse the masses of the people", will certainly perish.

Thus it is clear that there is no future for any Three People's Principles which depart from the Three Great Policies of alliance with Russia, co-operation with the Communist Party and assistance to the peasants and workers. Every conscientious follower of the Three People's Principles must seriously consider this point.

The Three People's Principles comprising the Three Great Policies — in other words, the revolutionary, new and genuine Three People's Principles — are the Three People's Principles of New Democracy, a development of the old Three People's Principles, a great contribution of Dr. Sun Yat-sen's and a product of the era in which the Chinese revolution has become part of the world socialist revolution. It is only these Three People's Principles which the Chinese Communist Party regards as "being what China needs today" and for whose "complete realization" it declares itself pledged "to fight". These are the only Three People's Principles which are in basic agreement with the Communist Party's political programme for the stage of democratic revolution, namely, with its minimum programme.

As for the old Three People's Principles, they were a product of the old period of the Chinese revolution. Russia was then an imperialist power, and naturally there could be no policy of alliance with her; there was then no Communist Party in existence in our country, and naturally there could be no policy of co-operation with it; the movement of the workers and peasants had not yet revealed its full political significance and aroused people's attention, and naturally there could be no policy of alliance with them. Hence the Three People's Principles of the period before the reorganization of the Kuomintang in 1924 belonged to the old category, and they became obsolete. The Kuomintang could not have gone forward unless it had developed them into the new Three People's Principles. Dr. Sun Yat-sen in his wisdom saw this point, secured the help of the Soviet Union and the Chinese Communist Party and reinterpreted the Three People's Principles so as to endow them with new characteristics suited to the times; as a result, a united front was formed between the Three People's Principles and communism, Kuomintang-Communist co-operation was established for the first time, the sympathy of the people of the whole country was won, and the revolution of 1924-27 was launched.

The old Three People's Principles were revolutionary in the old period and reflected its historical features. But if the old stuff is repeated in the new period after the new Three People's Principles have been established, or alliance with Russia is opposed after the socialist state has been established, or co-operation with the Communist Party is opposed after the Communist Party has come into existence, or the policy of assisting the peasants and workers is opposed after they have awakened and demonstrated their political strength, then that is reactionary and shows ignorance of the times. The period of reaction after 1927 was the result of such ignorance. The old proverb says, "Whosoever understands the signs of the times is a great man." I hope the followers of the Three People's Principles today will bear this in mind.

Were the Three People's Principles to fall within the old category, then they would have nothing basically in common with the communist minimum programme, because they would belong to the past and be obsolete. Any sort of Three People's Principles that oppose Russia, the Communist Party or the peasants and workers are definitely reactionary; they not only have absolutely nothing in common with the communist minimum programme but are the enemy of communism, and there is no common ground at all. This, too, the followers of the Three People's Principles should carefully consider.

In any case, people with a conscience will never forsake the new Three People's Principles until the task of opposing imperialism and feudalism is basically accomplished. The only ones who do are people like Wang Ching-wei. No matter how energetically they push their spurious Three People's Principles which oppose Russia, the Communist Party and the peasants and workers, there will surely be no lack of people with a conscience and sense of justice who will continue to support Sun Yat-sen's genuine Three People's Principles. Many followers of the genuine Three People's Principles continued the struggle for the Chinese revolution even after the reaction of 1927, and their numbers will undoubtedly swell to tens upon tens of thousands now that the national enemy has penetrated deep into our territory. We Communists will always persevere in long-term co-operation with all the true followers of the Three People's Principles and, while rejecting the traitors and the sworn enemies of communism, will never forsake any of our friends.

XI. THE CULTURE OF NEW DEMOCRACY

In the foregoing we have explained the historical characteristics of Chinese politics in the new period and the question of the new-democratic republic. We can now proceed to the question of culture.

A given culture is the ideological reflection of the politics and economics of a given society. There is in China an imperialist culture which is a reflection of imperialist rule, or partial rule, in the political and economic fields. This culture is fostered not only by the cultural organizations run directly by the imperialists in China but by a number of Chinese who have lost all sense of shame. Into this category falls all culture embodying a slave ideology. China also has a semifeudal culture which reflects her semi-feudal politics and economy, and whose exponents include all those who advocate the worship of Confucius, the study of the Confucian canon, the old ethical code and the old ideas in opposition to the new culture and new ideas. Imperialist culture and semi-feudal culture are devoted brothers and have formed a reactionary cultural alliance against China's new culture. This kind of reactionary culture serves the imperialists and the feudal class and must be swept away. Unless it is swept away, no new culture of any kind can be built up. There is no construction without destruction, no flowing without damming and no motion without rest; the two are locked in a life-and-death struggle.

99

As for the new culture, it is the ideological reflection of the new politics and the new economy which it sets out to serve.

As we have already stated in Section 3, Chinese society has gradually changed in character since the emergence of a capitalist economy in China; it is no longer an entirely feudal but a semi-feudal society, although the feudal economy still predominates. Compared with the feudal economy, this capitalist economy is a new one. The political forces of the bourgeoisie, the petty bourgeoisie and the proletariat are the new political forces which have emerged and grown simultaneously with this new capitalist economy. And the new culture reflects these new economic and political forces in the field of ideology and serves them. Without the capitalist economy, without the bourgeoisie, the petty bourgeoisie and the proletariat, and without the political forces of these classes, the new ideology or new culture could not have emerged.

These new political, economic and cultural forces are all revolutionary forces which are opposed to the old politics, the old economy and the old culture. The old is composed of two parts, one being China's own semi-feudal politics, economy and culture, and the other the politics, economy and culture of imperialism, with the latter heading the alliance. Both are bad and should be completely destroyed. The struggle between the new and the old in Chinese society is a struggle between the new forces of the people (the various revolutionary classes) and the old forces of imperialism and the feudal class. It is a struggle between revolution and counter-revolution. This struggle has lasted a full hundred years if dated from the Opium War, and nearly thirty years if dated from the Revolution of 1911.

But as already indicated, revolutions too can be classified into old and new, and what is new in one historical period becomes old in another. The century of China's bourgeois-democratic revolution can be divided into two main stages, a first stage of eighty years and a second of twenty years. Each has its basic historical characteristics: China's bourgeois-democratic revolution in the first eighty years belongs to the old category, while in the last twenty years, owing to the change in the international and domestic political situation, it belongs to the new category. Old democracy is the characteristic of the first eighty years. New Democracy is the characteristic of the last twenty. This distinction holds good in culture as well as in politics.

How does it manifest itself in the field of culture? We shall explain this next.

XII. THE HISTORICAL CHARACTERISTICS OF
CHINA'S CULTURAL REVOLUTION

On the cultural or ideological front, the two periods preceding and following the May 4th Movement form two distinct historical periods.

Before the May 4th Movement, the struggle on China's cultural front was one between the new culture of the bourgeoisie and the old culture of the feudal class. The struggles between the modern school system and the imperial examination system,[18] between the new learning and the old learning, and between Western learning and Chinese learning, were all of this nature. The so-called modern schools or new learning or Western learning of that time concentrated mainly (we say mainly, because in part pernicious vestiges of Chinese feudalism still remained) on the natural sciences and bourgeois social and political theories, which were needed by the representatives of the bourgeoisie. At the time, the ideology of the new learning played a revolutionary role in fighting the Chinese feudal ideology, and it served the bourgeois-democratic revolution of the old period. However, because the Chinese bourgeoisie lacked strength and the world had already entered the era of imperialism, this bourgeois ideology was only able to last out a few rounds and was beaten back by the reactionary alliance of the enslaving ideology of foreign imperialism and the "back to the ancients" ideology of Chinese feudalism; as soon as this reactionary ideological alliance started a minor counter-offensive, the so-called new learning lowered its banners, muffled its drums and beat a retreat, retaining its outer form but losing its soul. The old bourgeois-democratic culture became enervated and decayed in the era of imperialism, and its failure was inevitable.

But since the May 4th Movement things have been different. A brand-new cultural force came into being in China, that is, the communist culture and ideology guided by the Chinese Communists, or the communist world outlook and theory of social revolution. The May 4th Movement occurred in 1919, and in 1921 came the founding of the Chinese Communist Party and the real beginning of China's labour movement — all in the wake of the First World War and the October Revolution, *i.e.*, at a time when the national problem and the colonial revolutionary movements of the world underwent a change, and the connection between the Chinese revolution and the world

101

revolution became quite obvious. The new political force of the proletariat and the Communist Party entered the Chinese political arena, and as a result, the new cultural force, in new uniform and with new weapons, mustering all possible allies and deploying its ranks in battle array, launched heroic attacks on imperialist culture and feudal culture. This new force has made great strides in the domain of the social sciences and of the arts and letters, whether of philosophy, economics, political science, military science, history, literature or art (including the theatre, the cinema, music, sculpture and painting). For the last twenty years, wherever this new cultural force has directed its attack, a great revolution has taken place both in ideological content and in form (for example, in the written language). Its influence has been so great and its impact so powerful that it is invincible wherever it goes. The numbers it has rallied behind it have no parallel in Chinese history. Lu Hsun was the greatest and the most courageous standard-bearer of this new cultural force. The chief commander of China's cultural revolution, he was not only a great man of letters but a great thinker and revolutionary. Lu Hsun was a man of unyielding integrity, free from all sycophancy or obsequiousness; this quality is invaluable among colonial and semi-colonial peoples. Representing the great majority of the nation, Lu Hsun breached and stormed the enemy citadel; on the cultural front he was the bravest and most correct, the firmest, the most loyal and the most ardent national hero, a hero without parallel in our history. The road he took was the very road of China's new national culture.

Prior to the May 4th Movement, China's new culture was a culture of the old-democratic kind and part of the capitalist cultural revolution of the world bourgeoisie. Since the May 4th Movement, it has become new-democratic and part of the socialist cultural revolution of the world proletariat.

Prior to the May 4th Movement, China's new cultural movement, her cultural revolution, was led by the bourgeoisie, which still had a leading role to play. After the May 4th Movement, its culture and ideology became even more backward than its politics and were incapable of playing any leading role; at most, they could serve to a certain extent as an ally during revolutionary periods, while inevitably the responsibility for leading the alliance rested on proletarian culture and ideology. This is an undeniable fact.

The new-democratic culture is the anti-imperialist and anti-feudal culture of the broad masses; today it is the culture of the anti-Japanese united front. This culture can be led only by the culture and ideology of the proletariat, by the ideology of communism, and not by the culture and ideology of any other class. In a word, new-democratic culture is the proletarian-led, anti-imperialist and anti-feudal culture of the broad masses.

XIII.   THE FOUR PERIODS

A cultural revolution is the ideological reflection of the political and economic revolution and is in their service. In China there is a united front in the cultural as in the political revolution.

The history of the united front in the cultural revolution during the last twenty years can be divided into four periods. The first covers the two years from 1919 to 1921, the second the six years from 1921 to 1927, the third the ten years from 1927 to 1937, and the fourth the three years from 1937 to the present.

The first period extended from the May 4th Movement of 1919 to the founding of the Chinese Communist Party in 1921. The May 4th Movement was its chief landmark.

The May 4th Movement was an anti-imperialist as well as an anti-feudal movement. Its outstanding historical significance is to be seen in a feature which was absent from the Revolution of 1911, namely, its thorough and uncompromising opposition to imperialism as well as to feudalism. The May 4th Movement possessed this quality because capitalism had developed a step further in China and because new hopes had arisen for the liberation of the Chinese nation as China's revolutionary intellectuals saw the collapse of three great imperialist powers, Russia, Germany and Austria-Hungary, and the weakening of two others, Britain and France, while the Russian proletariat had established a socialist state and the German, Hungarian and Italian proletariat had risen in revolution. The May 4th Movement came into being at the call of the world revolution, of the Russian Revolution and of Lenin. It was part of the world proletarian revolution of the time. Although the Communist Party had not yet come into existence, there were already large numbers of intellectuals who approved of the Russian Revolution and had the rudiments of communist ideology. In the beginning the May 4th Movement was the revolutionary movement of a united front of three sections of people — communist intellectuals, revolutionary petty-bourgeois intellectuals and bourgeois intellectuals (the last forming the right wing of the movement). Its shortcoming was that it was confined to the intellectuals and that the workers and peasants did not join in. But as soon as it developed into the June 3rd Movement,[19] not only the intellectuals but the mass of the proletariat, the petty bourgeoisie and the bourgeoisie joined in, and it became a nation-wide revolutionary movement. The cultural revolution ushered in by the May 4th Movement was uncompromising in its opposition to feudal culture; there had never been such a great and thoroughgoing cultural revolution since the dawn of Chinese history. Raising aloft the two great banners of the day, "Down with the old ethics and up with the new!" and "Down with the old literature and up with the new!", the cultural revolution had great achievements to its credit. At that time it was not yet possible for this cultural movement to become widely diffused among the workers and peasants. The slogan of "Literature for the common people" was advanced, but in fact the "common people" then could only refer to the petty-bourgeois and bourgeois intellectuals in the cities, that is, the urban intelligentsia. Both in ideology and in the matter of cadres, the May 4th Movement paved the way for the founding of the Chinese Communist Party in 1921 and for the May 30th Movement in 1925 and the Northern Expedition. The bourgeois intellectuals, who constituted the right wing of the May 4th Movement, mostly compromised with the enemy in the second period and went over to the side of reaction.

In the second period, whose landmarks were the founding of the Chinese Communist Party, the May 30th Movement and the Northern Expedition, the united front of the three classes formed in the May 4th Movement was continued and expanded, the peasantry was drawn into it and a political united front of all these classes, the first instance of Kuomintang-Communist co-operation, was established. Dr. Sun Yat-sen was a great man not only because he led the great Revolution of 1911 (although it was only a democratic revolution of the old period), but also because, "adapting himself to the trends of the world and meeting the needs of the masses", he had the capacity to bring forward the revolutionary Three Great Policies of alliance with Russia, co-operation with the Communist Party and assistance to the peasants and workers, give new meaning to the Three People's Principles and thus institute the new Three People's Principles with their Three Great Policies. Previously, the Three People's Principles had exerted little influence on the educational and academic world or with the youth, because they had not raised the issues of opposition to imperialism or to the feudal social system and feudal culture and ideology. They were the old Three People's Principles which people regarded as the time-serving banner of a group of men bent on seizing power, in other words, on securing official positions, a banner used purely for political manoeuvring. Then came the new Three People's Principles with their Three Great Policies. The co-operation between the Kuomintang and the Communist Party and the joint efforts of the revolutionary members of the two parties spread the new Three People's Principles all over China, extending to a section of the educational and academic world and the mass of student youth. This was entirely due to the fact that the original Three People's Principles had developed into the anti-imperialist, anti-feudal and new-democratic Three People's Principles with their Three Great Policies. Without this development it would have been impossible to disseminate the ideas of the Three People's Principles.

During this period, the revolutionary Three People's Principles became the political basis of the united front of the Kuomintang and the Communist Party and of all the revolutionary classes, and since "communism is the good friend of the Three People's Principles", a united front was formed between the two of them. In terms of social classes, it was a united front of the proletariat, the peasantry, the urban petty bourgeoisie and the bourgeoisie. Using the Communist *Weekly Guide*, the Kuomintang's *Republican Daily News* of Shanghai and other newspapers in various localities as their bases of operations, the two parties jointly advocated anti-imperialism, jointly combated feudal education based upon the worship of Confucius and upon the study of the Confucian canon and jointly opposed feudal literature and the classical language and promoted the new literature and the vernacular style of writing with an anti-imperialist and anti-feudal content. During the wars in Kwangtung and during the Northern Expedition, they reformed China's armed forces by the inculcation of anti-imperialist and anti-feudal ideas. The slogans, "Down with the corrupt officials" and "Down with the local tyrants and evil gentry", were raised among the peasant millions, and great peasant revolutionary struggles were aroused. Thanks to all this and to the assistance of the Soviet Union, the Northern Expedition was victorious. But no sooner did the big bourgeoisie climb to power than it put an end to this revolution, thus creating an entirely new political situation.

The third period was the new revolutionary period of 1927-37. As a change had taken place within the revolutionary camp towards the end of the second period, with the big bourgeoisie going over to the counter-revolutionary camp of the imperialist and feudal forces and the national bourgeoisie trailing after it, only three of the four classes formerly within the revolutionary camp remained, *i.e.*, the proletariat, the peasantry and the other sections of the petty bourgeoisie (including the revolutionary intellectuals), and consequently the Chinese revolution inevitably entered a new period in which the Chinese Communist Party alone gave leadership to the masses. This period was one of counter-revolutionary campaigns of "encirclement and suppression", on the one hand, and of the deepening of the revolution, on the other. There were two kinds of counter-revolutionary campaigns of "encirclement and suppression", the military and the cultural. The deepening of the revolution was of two kinds; both the agrarian and the cultural revolutions were deepened. At the instigation of the imperialists, the counter-revolutionary forces of the whole country and of the whole world were mobilized for both kinds of campaigns of "encirclement and suppression", which lasted no less than ten years and were unparalleled in their ruthlessness; hundreds of thousands of Communists and young students were slaughtered and millions of workers and peasants suffered cruel persecution. The people responsible for all this apparently had no doubt that communism and the Communist Party could be "exterminated once and for all". However, the outcome was different; both kinds of "encirclement and suppression" campaigns failed miserably. The military campaign resulted in the northern march of the Red Army to resist the Japanese, and the cultural campaign resulted in the outbreak of the December 9th Movement of the revolutionary youth in 1935. And the common result of both was the awakening of the people of the whole country. These were three positive results. The most amazing thing of all was that the Kuomintang's cultural "encirclement and suppression" campaign failed completely in the Kuomintang areas as well, although the Communist Party was in an utterly defenceless position in all the cultural and educational institutions there. Why did this happen? Does it not give food for prolonged and deep thought? It was in the very midst of such campaigns of "encirclement and suppression" that Lu Hsun, who believed in communism, became the giant of China's cultural revolution.

The negative result of the counter-revolutionary campaigns of "encirclement and suppression" was the invasion of our country by

106

Japanese imperialism. This is the chief reason why to this very day the people of the whole country still bitterly detest those ten years of anti-communism.

In the struggles of this period, the revolutionary side firmly upheld the people's anti-imperialist and anti-feudal New Democracy and their new Three People's Principles, while the counter-revolutionary side, under the direction of imperialism, imposed the despotic regime of the coalition of the landlord class and the big bourgeoisie. That despotic regime butchered Dr. Sun Yat-sen's Three Great Policies and his new Three People's Principles both politically and culturally, with catastrophic consequences to the Chinese nation.

The fourth period is that of the present anti-Japanese war. Pursuing its zigzag course, the Chinese revolution has again arrived at a united front of the four classes; but the scope of the united front is now much broader because its upper stratum includes many members of the ruling classes, its middle stratum includes the national bourgeoisie and the petty bourgeoisie, and its lower stratum includes the entire proletariat, so that the various classes and strata of the nation have become members of the alliance resolutely resisting Japanese imperialism. The first stage of this period lasted until the fall of Wuhan. During that stage, there was a lively atmosphere in the country in every field; politically there was a trend towards democracy and culturally there was fairly widespread activity. With the fall of Wuhan the second stage began, during which the political situation has undergone many changes, with one section of the big bourgeoisie capitulating to the enemy and another desiring an early end to the War of Resistance. In the cultural sphere, this situation has been reflected in the reactionary activities of Yeh Ching,[20] Chang Chun-mai and others, and in the suppression of freedom of speech and of the press.

To overcome this crisis, a firm struggle is necessary against all ideas opposed to resistance, unity and progress, and unless these reactionary ideas are crushed, there will be no hope of victory. How will this struggle turn out? This is the big question in the minds of the people of the whole country. Judging by the domestic and international situation, the Chinese people are bound to win, however numerous the obstacles on the path of resistance. The progress achieved during the twenty years since the May 4th Movement exceeds not only that of the preceding eighty years but virtually surpasses that achieved in the thousands of years of Chinese history. Can we not visualize what further progress China will make in another twenty years? The unbridled violence of all the forces of darkness, whether domestic or foreign, has brought disaster to our nation; but this very violence indicates that while the forces of darkness still have some strength left, they are already in their death throes, and that the people are gradually approaching victory. This is true of China, of the whole East and of the entire world.

XIV. SOME WRONG IDEAS ABOUT THE NATURE OF CULTURE

Everything new comes from the forge of hard and bitter struggle. This is also true of the new culture which has followed a zigzag course in the past twenty years, during which both the good and the bad were tested and proved in struggle.

The bourgeois die-hards are as hopelessly wrong on the question of culture as on that of political power. They neither understand the historical characteristics of this new period in China, nor recognize the new-democratic culture of the masses. Their starting point is bourgeois despotism, which in culture becomes the cultural despotism of the bourgeoisie. It seems that a section (and I refer only to a section) of educated people from the so-called European-American school[21] who in fact supported the Kuomintang government's "Communist suppression" campaign on the cultural front in the past are now supporting its policy of "restricting" and "corroding" the Communist Party. They do not want the workers and the peasants to hold up their heads politically or culturally. This bourgeois die-hard road of cultural despotism leads nowhere; as in the case of political despotism, the domestic and international pre-conditions are lacking. Therefore this cultural despotism, too, had better be "folded up".

So far as the orientation of our national culture is concerned, communist ideology plays the guiding role, and we should work hard both to disseminate socialism and communism throughout the working class and to educate the peasantry and other sections of the people in socialism properly and step by step. However, our national culture as a whole is not yet socialist.

Because of the leadership of the proletariat, the politics, the economy and the culture of New Democracy all contain an element of socialism, and by no means a mere casual element but one with a decisive role. However, taken as a whole, the political, economic and cultural situation so far is new-democratic and not socialist. For the Chinese revolution in its present stage is not yet a socialist revolution for the overthrow of capitalism but a bourgeois-democratic revolution, its central task being mainly that of combating foreign imperialism and domestic feudalism. In the sphere of national culture, it is wrong to assume that the existing national culture is, or should be, socialist in its entirety. That would amount to confusing the dissemination of communist ideology with the carrying out of an immediate programme of action, and to confusing the application of the communist standpoint and method in investigating problems, undertaking research, handling work and training cadres with the general policy for national education and national culture in the democratic stage of the Chinese revolution. A national culture with a socialist content will necessarily be the reflection of a socialist politics and a socialist economy. There are socialist elements in our politics and our economy, and hence these socialist elements are reflected in our national culture; but taking our society as a whole, we do not have a socialist politics and a socialist economy yet, so that there cannot be a wholly socialist national culture. Since the present Chinese revolution is part of the world proletarian-socialist revolution, the new culture of China today is part of the world proletarian-socialist new culture and is its great ally. While this part contains vital elements of socialist culture, the national culture as a whole joins the stream of the world proletarian-socialist new culture not entirely as a socialist culture, but as the anti-imperialist and anti-feudal new-democratic culture of the broad masses. And since the Chinese revolution today cannot do without proletarian leadership, China's new culture cannot do without the leadership of proletarian culture and ideology, of communist ideology. At the present stage, however, this kind of leadership means leading the masses of the people in an anti-imperialist and anti-feudal political and cultural revolution, and therefore, taken as a whole, the content of China's new national culture is still not socialist but new-democratic.

Beyond all doubt, now is the time to spread communist ideas more widely and put more energy into the study of Marxism-Leninism, or otherwise we shall not only be unable to lead the Chinese revolution forward to the future stage of socialism, but shall also be unable to guide the present democratic revolution to victory. However, we must keep the spreading of communist ideas and propaganda about the communist social system distinct from the practical application of the new-democratic programme of action; we must also keep the communist theory and method of investigating problems, undertaking research, handling work and training cadres distinct from the new-democratic line for national culture as a whole. It is undoubtedly inappropriate to mix the two up.

It can thus be seen that the content of China's new national culture at the present stage is neither the cultural despotism of the bourgeoisie nor the socialism of the proletariat, but the anti-imperialist and anti-feudal New Democracy of the masses, under the leadership of proletarian-socialist culture and ideology.

XV. A NATIONAL, SCIENTIFIC AND MASS CULTURE

New-democratic culture is national. It opposes imperialist oppression and upholds the dignity and independence of the Chinese nation. It belongs to our own nation and bears our own national characteristics. It links up with the socialist and new-democratic cultures of all other nations and they are related in such a way that they can absorb something from each other and help each other to develop, together forming a new world culture; but as a revolutionary national culture it can never link up with any reactionary imperialist culture of whatever nation. To nourish her own culture China needs to assimilate a good deal of foreign progressive culture, not enough of which was done in the past. We should assimilate whatever is useful to us today not only from the present-day socialist and new-democratic cultures but also from the earlier cultures of other nations, for example, from the culture of the various capitalist countries in the Age of Enlightenment. However, we should not gulp any of this foreign material down uncritically, but must treat it as we do our food — first chewing it, then submitting it to the working of the stomach and intestines with their juices and secretions, and separating it into nutriment to be absorbed and waste matter to be discarded — before it can nourish us. To advocate "wholesale westernization"[22] is wrong. China has suffered a great deal from the mechanical absorption of foreign material. Similarly, in applying Marxism to China, Chinese communists must fully and properly integrate the universal truth of Marxism with the concrete practice of the Chinese revolution, or in

110

other words, the universal truth of Marxism must be combined with specific national characteristics and acquire a definite national form if it is to be useful, and in no circumstances can it be applied subjectively as a mere formula. Marxists who make a fetish of formulas are simply playing the fool with Marxism and the Chinese revolution, and there is no room for them in the ranks of the Chinese revolution. Chinese culture should have its own form, its own national form. National in form and new-democratic in content — such is our new culture today.

New-democratic culture is scientific. Opposed as it is to all feudal and superstitious ideas, it stands for seeking truth from facts, for objective truth and for the unity of theory and practice. On this point, the possibility exists of a united front against imperialism, feudalism and superstition between the scientific thought of the Chinese proletariat and those Chinese bourgeois materialists and natural scientists who are progressive, but in no case is there a possibility of a united front with any reactionary idealism. In the field of political action Communists may form an anti-imperialist and anti-feudal united front with some idealists and even religious people, but we can never approve of their idealism or religious doctrines. A splendid old culture was created during the long period of Chinese feudal society. To study the development of this old culture, to reject its feudal dross and assimilate its democratic essence is a necessary condition for developing our new national culture and increasing our national self-confidence, but we should never swallow anything and everything uncritically. It is imperative to separate the fine old culture of the people which had a more or less democratic and revolutionary character from all the decadence of the old feudal ruling class. China's present new politics and new economy have developed out of her old politics and old economy, and her present new culture, too, has developed out of her old culture; therefore, we must respect our own history and must not lop it off. However, respect for history means giving it its proper place as a science, respecting its dialectical development, and not eulogizing the past at the expense of the present or praising every drop of feudal poison. As far as the masses and the young students are concerned, the essential thing is to guide them to look forward and not backward.

New-democratic culture belongs to the broad masses and is therefore democratic. It should serve the toiling masses of workers and peasants who make up more than 90 per cent of the nation's population and should gradually become their very own. There is a difference of degree, as well as a close link, between the knowledge imparted to

111

the revolutionary cadres and the knowledge imparted to the revolutionary masses, between the raising of cultural standards and popularization. Revolutionary culture is a powerful revolutionary weapon for the broad masses of the people. It prepares the ground ideologically before the revolution comes and is an important, indeed essential, fighting front in the general revolutionary front during the revolution. People engaged in revolutionary cultural work are the commanders at various levels on this cultural front. "Without revolutionary theory there can be no revolutionary movement",[23] one can thus see how important the cultural movement is for the practical revolutionary movement. Both the cultural and practical movements must be of the masses. Therefore all progressive cultural workers in the anti-Japanese war must have their own cultural battalions, that is, the broad masses. A revolutionary cultural worker who is not close to the people is a commander without an army, whose fire-power cannot bring the enemy down. To attain this objective, written Chinese must be reformed, given the requisite conditions, and our spoken language brought closer to that of the people, for the people, it must be stressed, are the inexhaustible source of our revolutionary culture.

A national, scientific and mass culture — such is the anti-imperialist and anti-feudal culture of the people, the culture of New Democracy, the new culture of the Chinese nation.

Combine the politics, the economy and the culture of New Democracy, and you have the new-democratic republic, the Republic of China both in name and in reality, the new China we want to create.

Behold, New China is within sight. Let us all hail her!

Her masts have already risen above the horizon. Let us all cheer in welcome!

Raise both your hands. New China is ours!

NOTES

[1] *Chinese Culture* was a magazine founded in January 1940 in Yenan; the present article appeared in the first number.

[2] See V. I. Lenin, "Once Again on the Trade Unions, the Present Situation and the Mistakes of Trotsky and Bukharin", *Selected Works*, Eng. ed., International Publishers, New York, 1943, Vol. IX, p. 54.

[3] Karl Marx, "Preface to *A Contribution to the Critique of Political Economy*", *Selected Works of Marx and Engels*, Eng. ed., FLPH, Moscow, 1958, Vol. I, p. 363.

[4] Karl Marx, "Theses on Feuerbach", *Selected Works of Marx and Engels*, Eng. ed., FLPH, Moscow, 1958, Vol. II, p. 405.

[5] J. V. Stalin, "The October Revolution and the National Question", *Works*, Eng. ed., FLPH, Moscow, 1953, Vol. IV, pp. 169-70.

[6] J. V. Stalin, "The National Question Once Again", *Works*, Eng. ed., FLPH, Moscow, 1954, Vol. VII, pp. 225-27.

[7] V. I. Lenin, "Imperialism, the Highest Stage of Capitalism", *Selected Works*, Eng. ed., FLPH, Moscow, 1950, Vol. I, Part 2, p. 566.

[8] These anti-Soviet campaigns were instigated by the Kuomintang government following Chiang Kai-shek's betrayal of the revolution. On December 13, 1927, the Kuomintang murdered the Soviet vice-consul in Canton and on the next day its government in Nanking issued a decree breaking off relations with Russia, withdrawing official recognition from Soviet consuls in the provinces and ordering Soviet commercial establishments to cease activity. In August 1929 Chiang Kai-shek, under the instigation of the imperialists, organized acts of provocation in the Northeast against the Soviet Union, which resulted in armed clashes.

[9] After World War I the British imperialists instigated their vassal Greece to commit aggression against Turkey, but the Turkish people, with the help of the Soviet Union, defeated the Greek troops in 1922. In 1923, Kemal was elected President of Turkey. Stalin said:

> A Kemalist revolution is a revolution of the top stratum, a revolution of the national merchant bourgeoisie, arising in a struggle against the foreign imperialists, and whose subsequent development is essentially directed against the peasants and workers, against the very possibility of an agrarian revolution. ("Talk with Students of the Sun Yat-sen University", *Works*, Eng. ed., FLPH, Moscow, 1954, Vol. IX, p. 261.)

[10] The "metaphysics-mongers" were Chang Chun-mai and his group. After the May 4th Movement, Chang openly opposed science and advocated metaphysics, or what he called "spiritual culture", and thus came to be known as a "metaphysics-monger". In order to support Chiang Kai-shek and the Japanese aggressors, he published an "Open Letter to Mr. Mao Tse-tung" in December 1938 at Chiang Kai-shek's bidding, wildly demanding the abolition of the Eighth Route Army, the New Fourth Army and the Shensi-Kansu-Ningsia Border Region.

[11] See the manifesto of the Central Committee of the Chinese Communist Party on the establishment of Kuomintang-Communist co-operation, issued in September 1937.

[12] See Dr. Sun Yat-sen, *Lectures on the Principle of People's Livelihood*, 1924, Lecture II.

[13] *Vitalism* was an exposition of Kuomintang fascism, a hotch-potch ghost-written by a number of reactionary hacks for Chen Li-fu, one of the notorious chiefs of Chiang Kai-shek's secret service.

[14] The "doctrine of distribution according to labour" was a high-sounding slogan shamelessly put forward by Yen Hsi-shan, warlord and representative of the big landlords and big compradors in Shansi Province.

[15] "Fight Against Attacks from Both Sides" was the title of an article written by Wang Ching-wei after his betrayal of the revolution in 1927.

[16] J. V. Stalin, "Concerning the National Question in Yugoslavia", a speech delivered in the Yugoslav Commission of the E.C.C.I., March 30, 1925. Stalin said:

> . . . the peasantry constitutes the main army of the national movement, . . . there is no powerful national movement without the peasant army, nor can

113

there be. That is what is meant when it is said that, *in essence*, the national question is a peasant question. (*Works*, Eng. ed., FLPH, Moscow, 1954, Vol. VII, pp. 71-72.)

[17] The "principle of going up into the hills" was a dogmatist gibe against Comrade Mao Tse-tung for his emphasis on rural revolutionary bases. He makes use of the expression to explain the importance of the role played by the rural revolutionary bases.

[18] The modern school system was the educational system modelled on that of capitalist countries in Europe and America. The imperial examination system was the old examination system in feudal China. Towards the end of the 19th century, enlightened Chinese intellectuals urged the abolition of the old competitive examination system and the establishment of modern schools.

[19] The June 3rd Movement marked a new stage in the patriotic movement of May 4. On June 3, 1919, students in Peking held public meetings and made speeches in defiance of persecution and repression by the army and police. They went on strike and the strike spread to the workers and merchants in Shanghai, Nanking, Tientsin, Hangchow, Wuhan and Kiukiang and in the provinces of Shantung and Anhwei. Thus the May 4th Movement grew into a broad mass movement in which the proletariat, the urban petty bourgeoisie and the national bourgeoisie all participated.

[20] Yeh Ching was a renegade Communist who became a hired hack in the Kuomintang secret service.

[21] The spokesman of the so-called European-American school was the counter-revolutionary Hu Shih.

[22] Wholesale westernization was the view held by a number of westernized Chinese bourgeois intellectuals who unconditionally praised the outmoded individualist bourgeois culture of the West and advocated the servile imitation of capitalist Europe and America.

[23] V. I. Lenin, "What Is to Be Done?", *Collected Works*, Eng. ed., FLPH, Moscow, 1961, Vol. V, p. 369.